THE LUNAR TIDE

Kanav Sachdev

White Light Publication

The characters and events portrayed in this book are fictitious. Any similarity to real persons, living or dead, is coincidental and not intended by the author.

ISBN-13: 978-81-999131-8-9 (Hardcover)
ISBN-13: 978-81-999131-9-6 (paperback)
ISBN-13: 978-81-998493-5-8 (Ebook)
ISBN-13: 978-81-999131-5-8 (Audio book)

Cover design by: Jyoti Kanav Sachdeva

To my Mother.....

If Father was the Sun that lit the path, You were the Water that sustained the journey. The Sun gives life, but the Moon makes life livable.

You taught me that a King without a heart is just a tyrant, And a Chariot without a destination is just a cage. Father built the walls of the house; you made it a Home.

This volume is the reflection of your peace.

CONTENTS

PREFACE

A LETTER FROM THE CHRIOTEER TO THE READER

This book was not written in a single sitting. It was written across a thousand midnights, when the world outside was quiet enough for the deeper questions to rise to the surface.

Why do brilliant men suffer? Why does a King with everything weep in the dark? Why does the most logical person in the room make the most disastrous emotional decisions? These are not abstract questions. They are the questions I heard at kitchen tables, in boardrooms, in hushed hospital corridors, and in the brittle silences between couples who had once loved fiercely and now could barely look at each other.

Volume 1 of The Charioteer's Code taught us the grammar of power—the Sun, Saturn, Jupiter, and Mars as the pillars of structure, duty, and authority. We built the Chariot. We understood the engine and the wheels. But once the structure was in place, a deeper ache remained. The Kings were restless. The Chariots stood polished and ready, yet the drivers refused to move.

The answer lay not in the hard planets of governance but in the liquid planets of feeling. It lay in the Moon and in Venus. It lay in the tides.

Volume 2: The Lunar Tide is the chemistry of the soul. It is the study of how peace is manufactured and how desire is forged. Drawing from the ancient, cryptic wisdom of the Lal Kitab—the Red Book of Vedic astrology—this volume decodes the two forces that silently govern the inner life of every human being: the Mind (Chandra) and the Desire (Shukra).

You will find that the Lal Kitab is no ordinary astrological text. It does not traffic in fatalism. It insists, with revolutionary boldness, that destiny is not merely inherited but can be synthesized. That a weak Moon can be manufactured using the Sun and Jupiter. That a broken Venus can be repaired by understanding the dance of Rahu and Ketu. That the remedy for a sleepless night may not be a gemstone but a behavioral alignment—a bow before a teacher, a glass of water drawn from silver, a blue flower buried quietly in the earth.

The Dialogue between Aruna the Charioteer and Surya the Sun—which forms the narrative spine of this book—is my way of making this ancient science approachable. Surya does not lecture; he illuminates. Aruna does not just receive wisdom; he challenges it, because I believe the reader deserves to challenge it too.
This book is for the restless King who has achieved everything and feels nothing. For the devoted partner who cannot understand why love keeps running through their fingers. For the seeker who suspects that the rituals they perform have a logic deeper than superstition. And for the astrologer or student who wishes to look beneath the surface of a chart and read not just the positions of planets, but the chemistry between them.

The journey from Volume 1 to Volume 2 is the journey from the Throne Room to the Private Chambers. From the architecture of power to the alchemy of feeling. Read slowly. The tides do not rush.

Kanav Sachdev
2026

PROLOGUE

THE REFLECTION IN THE WATER

Somewhere above the burning plains of the first journey,the Celestial Chariot crests a ridge—and for the first time, Aruna sees water.

The first volume had been a country of hard things. Bone and iron. The architecture of thrones. The geometry of power. Aruna the Charioteer had learned to read the politics of the sky—to see the Sun as the King, Saturn as the cold-eyed Judge, Mars as the soldier who asks no questions and carries all wounds. He had mapped the skeleton of destiny and found it magnificent in its severity.

But skeletons do not bleed.

Now, cresting the ridge, Aruna sees the land change below him. The hard, sun-baked clay of the first terrain gives way to something silver and yielding. Rivers. Lakes. Tidal estuaries where the salt of the sea meets the sweetness of the mountain stream. The air smells different here—softer, faintly jasmine-scented, carrying the distant sound of women's laughter and the particular silence that gathers in rooms where children sleep.

He turns to Surya, who drives the Chariot with the unhurried confidence of someone who has crossed this border a thousand times.

"O Surya," Aruna says slowly, "I have studied Kings who weep and Scholars who starve. I have seen Generals who cannot sleep and Priests who rot from the inside. We treated the bones, and the patient still bled. We fixed the Engine. We greased the Wheels. Yet the Charioteer kept dying at the reins. What affliction did we miss?"

Surya does not look at him. He looks at the water below, and his face—always so incandescent, so impossible to stare at directly—softens into something that resembles tenderness.

"You fixed the container," Surya says. "You forgot the contents. A Chariot made of solid gold is a tomb if the driver is dying of thirst."

Aruna is quiet for a long moment. Below them, a river bends around a village. Lamplight flickers in windows. A woman stands on a veranda looking at the night sky with an expression that is not prayer exactly, but is close to it.
"The Moon," Aruna says at last. Not a question.

"The Moon," Surya confirms. "And what the Moon carries in its tide."

This is the country they are entering. Not the country of Kings and Courts but the country of private rooms and midnight thoughts. Not the jurisprudence of Saturn but the chemistry of Chandra. Not the fire that builds empires but the water that makes empires worth building.
In the Lal Kitab—that cryptic, irreverent, deeply human Red Book—there are two forces that are said to determine not what a person achieves, but whether they can feel the achievement. The Moon, which governs the mind and the mother and the liquid wealth of a life. And Venus, which governs desire, beauty, the beloved, and the body's deepest hungers.

These are the forces that cannot be seen in a balance sheet. They cannot be measured by the size of a throne or the number of horses in the stable. They are the difference between a house and a home. Between a contract and a marriage. Between a life that is impressive and a life that is lived.

The Chariot descends toward the water.

The Lunar Tide has begun.

DISCLAIMER

Please read this disclaimer carefully before using this book or applying any of the principles described herein.

Fictionalization and Privacy

The case studies, anecdotes, and personal stories presented within this book are included for educational and illustrative purposes only. While they are inspired by real-world concepts and experiences, they are fictionalized. In all instances, the names, identifying details, professions, locations, and other key details of individuals have been altered or entirely fabricated to protect privacy and ensure anonymity. Any resemblance to actual persons, living or dead, or actual events is purely coincidental.

Not Professional Advice

The content of the book is intended to provide information, spiritual concepts, and personal development principles based on the author's interpretation of ancient texts and practices. It is not intended to be a substitute for professional medical advice, diagnosis, or treatment.

- Consult a Professional: Always seek the advice of your physician or other qualified health provider with any questions you may have regarding a medical condition or before undertaking any new breathing or physical practice, particularly those involving breath retention or physical implements (such as the Yoga Danda).

- Use at Your Own Risk: The practices described in this book should be approached with respect and caution. The author and publisher are not responsible for any adverse effects or consequences resulting from the use of any suggestions, practices, or preparations mentioned in this book. Your engagement with the material is entirely at your own risk.

THE REFLECTION IN THE WATER

Aruna: "O Surya, King of the Grahas, I have returned to the helm. We have traversed the burning plains of the First Volume. We have mapped the chassis of the Chariot, the fire of the engine, and the heavy iron wheels of Justice. I have mastered the grammar of heat and gravity. Yet, as I look down from the heavens upon the Earth, I see a strange and troubling paradox."

Surya: "Speak, Charioteer. The eyes of the driver must be sharper than the arrows of the warrior. What flaw do you see in the design of men?"

Aruna: "I see men who possess the solid Gold of Jupiter and the blazing Authority of the Sun. They sit on thrones of mahogany, their granaries are full to bursting, and their enemies have been vanquished by the weight of their command. By the laws of our first ledger, they should be complete. They have Structure. They have Duty. They have Power.

"Yet, at night, when the court is silent, these Kings pace their marble floors, unable to sleep. Their eyes are hollow, as if drained of light. Their breath is shallow, as if the air itself refuses to enter them. They have everything, O Sun, yet they feel they have nothing. Why is a man with a Golden Chariot miserable? Why does the King weep when the court is empty? Is the Chariot flawed?"

Surya turned his gaze away from the fire of the stars and looked toward the cool, silver horizon.

Surya: "You confuse *Structure* with *Substance*, Aruna. You are looking at the Chariot's frame, but you have forgotten the Charioteer's blood. You have studied the Engine, but you have ignored the Coolant. A Chariot made of solid gold is a tomb if the driver is dying of thirst. The Sun is the Engine; it provides the heat to move. Jupiter is the Air; it provides the breath to expand. But the Moon... the Moon is the Water. It is the coolant in the engine. It is the blood in the veins. It is the liquid cash in the pocket. It is the silence between the heartbeats."

Aruna: "But Water is soft, Surya. Water is yielding. How can it hold equal weight to the Fire of the Spirit?"

Surya: "Fire creates. Water sustains. Without the Sun, life cannot begin. But without the Moon, life cannot continue. The Sun defines who you *are*. The Moon defines how you *feel* about who you are. What use is a Kingdom if the King's mind is a storm? What use is Authority if there is no sweetness in the voice? You have learned the Physics of the Spirit. Now you must learn its Chemistry. In this Volume, we leave the formal Court of the King and enter the Private Chambers of the Soul. We discuss the *Lunar Tide*. We discuss the **Moon**—which is the Mind and the Mother—and **Venus**—which is the Desire and the Wife. Prepare yourself, Charioteer. The logic of Fire was straight and rigid; the logic of Water is fluid and deep. We must now learn to navigate the tides without drowning."

PART I: THE GRAMMAR OF TIDES

(Planetary Mechanics & Artificial Alchemy)

CHAPTER 1: THE MOLECULAR MOON

(The Alchemical Equation: Sun + Jupiter = Moon)

The Hidden Laboratory Of The Red Book

In the first volume of our journey, we approached the horoscope as a political map. We treated the planets as Sovereigns—Kings, Queens, Commanders, and Judges—sitting in their respective houses, exercising their jurisdiction. We studied their positions like pieces on a chessboard, calculating angles of sight, lines of defense, and degrees of power. This was necessary to build the foundation. We learned that the Sun is the King, Saturn is the Judge, and Mars is the Warrior.

But the *Lal Kitab* is not merely a study of celestial politics; it is a study of celestial *chemistry*.

Deep within the cryptic verses of the Red Book—buried beneath the remedies for throwing copper in rivers or feeding dogs—lies a concept that separates this text from all other astrological systems in the world. This is the concept of *Masnui Grah* (Artificial Planets).

Traditional astrology teaches us that the planets are static. A Moon is a Moon. A Sun is a Sun. They are immutable rocks floating in the void, casting their rays upon us. But the *Lal Kitab* opens the door to a "Hidden Laboratory." It postulates that planetary energies are not just dead weight; they are reactive elements. They are ingredients.

Just as Hydrogen and Oxygen—two invisible, dry gases—can collide to create Water, a substance entirely different from its parents, specific planetary combinations can be mixed to "manufacture" a new energy entirely. This implies a staggering truth: **Destiny is not just inherited; it can be synthesized.**

If a person is born with a weak Moon—destined for anxiety, poverty of liquid cash, or a lack of peace—they are not doomed to suffer forever. The *Lal Kitab* provides the formula to *manufacture* the Moon energy using other planets available in the chart. We can create "Artificial Water" if we know the recipe.

This chapter addresses the most fundamental crisis of the modern age: the crisis of Peace. To understand the Moon, we must stop looking at it as a satellite in the sky and start seeing it as a *chemical condition* created by the soul.

The Dialogue: The Recipe For Water

Aruna: "This confuses me, Surya. The Moon is a primary luminary. It is the Queen. It governs the tides of the ocean, the cycles of the mother, and the flow of blood. It is the 'white glare' that illuminates the night. How can such a fundamental force be 'manufactured'? Does the Moon not exist on its own?"

Surya: "In the celestial sphere, yes, the Moon is an independent body. It has its own mass and gravity. But in the human psyche—the internal Chariot—what you call 'The Moon' is actually 'Peace of Mind.' And Peace, Aruna, is not a raw ingredient. Peace is a *result.* Peace is what remains when the other forces are in balance. Tell me, Charioteer, look at the physical world. How do you create rain? How do you create the cloud?"

Aruna: "It is a cycle, O Light. Heat evaporates the water, it rises into the air, condenses, and falls back down."

Surya: "Correct. It requires Heat and Air. Without Heat, the water stays stagnant on the ground. Without Air, the vapor cannot rise and expand. Now, apply this to the planets. What is the ultimate Source of Heat in the chart?"

Aruna: "You are, O Sun. You are the Fire. You are the Atma (Soul)."

Surya: "And what is the ultimate Source of Air, Breath, and Expansion?"

Aruna: "Brihaspati (Jupiter). He is the Ether. He is the Expansion. He is the Breath of the Cosmos."

Surya: "Precisely. Now, write this equation in the center of your ledger, for it is the secret to all tranquility: **Sun + Jupiter = Moon.**"

Aruna: "Fire and Air create Water? The King (Sun) and the Priest

(Jupiter) create the Mother (Moon)? This contradicts the laws of the material world. Fire dries up water; Air scatters it. How can they create it? It seems paradoxical."

Surya: "It contradicts the laws of matter, but it follows the absolute laws of the Spirit. The **Sun** is the Ego, the Spine, the 'I am.' It is the stiff backbone of self-respect. **Jupiter** is the Dharma, the Breath, the 'I understand.' It is the wisdom that sees the larger pattern. When the fierce Authority of the Soul (Sun) is tempered by the oxygen of Divine Wisdom (Jupiter), a specific condensation occurs in the human heart. The heat of the ego is cooled by grace. The ambition is softened by understanding. This condensation—this cool, liquid state of being—is what you call 'The Moon.' When a man knows who he is (Sun) and understands his duty to the cosmos (Jupiter), he enters a state of flow. That flow is the Moon. Therefore, Aruna, if a passenger comes to you crying of sleepless nights, do not look at their Moon sign alone. Do not look for the Moon in the 4th House. Look at their Sun and their Jupiter. Has the King lost his dignity? Or has the Priest lost his faith?"

The Decoding: Manufacturing Peace

This concept of *Masnui Grah* completely overturns the standard diagnostic approach of Vedic astrology. Usually, if a client complains of depression or anxiety, the astrologer looks immediately at the Moon or the 4th House. If the Moon is afflicted by Saturn (Fear) or Rahu (Illusion), they prescribe Pearl or Silver.

But often, these remedies fail. The Pearl cracks, or the anxiety returns. Why?

The *Lal Kitab* suggests deeper pathology. It suggests that "Moon problems"—such as anxiety, insomnia, depression, and liquidity crunches—are often not problems with the Moon at all. They are problems of **Misaligned Sovereignty**. The factory that produces peace has shut down.

To "fix" the Moon, we must act as alchemists and repair its component parts. We must fix the Generator (Sun) and the Filter (Jupiter).

1. The Ingredient Analysis

To understand why this equation works, we must analyze the ingredients in their raw form. We must understand the *metaphysics* of these two giants.

Ingredient A: The Sun (The Structural Self) The Sun is the dry heat of self-respect. It is the Father, the Government, and the Spine. It is the container. Imagine a clay pot. The Sun is the fire that hardens the clay. If the Sun is weak, the pot is unbaked and brittle. It cannot hold water. A person with a weak Sun (low self-esteem, lack of discipline, weak father figure, or a compromised moral spine) cannot hold onto peace because they lack the structural integrity of the self. They are like a sieve; the water of peace pours right through them. They are porous to the world's insults. Every criticism breaks them. Without a strong "I am" (Sun), there can be no "I feel" (Moon).

Ingredient B: Jupiter (The Oxygen of Grace) Jupiter is the *Guru*, the breathable air, the expansion of the soul. It represents the ability to see the "Big Picture," to forgive, and to understand the moral law. It is the breath that cools the blood. Without Jupiter, the Sun is just a tyrant—hot, burning, and destructive. A King without Wisdom is a danger to his people. He burns the kingdom with his ego. He sees enemies everywhere because he lacks the vision (Jupiter) to see friends. Jupiter provides the "cooling wisdom" that turns the Sun's raw power into benevolent leadership. Jupiter turns "Force" into "Grace."

The Reaction: The Moon (Peace) When the *Structure* (Sun) is filled with *Grace* (Jupiter), the byproduct is *Satisfaction* (Moon). This is why the *Lal Kitab* states that if the Sun and Jupiter are well-placed and aspecting each other (e.g., Sun in 1st, Jupiter in

5th), the Moon is automatically rectified, even if the Moon itself is in a difficult house like the 6th or 8th. The factory is working; therefore, the product is being delivered. The person will always find peace, even in war.

2. The Diagnostic Parables

The best way to understand this alchemy is not through theory, but through the observation of human lives. When a "Passenger" enters your court complaining of mental turbulence, do not rush to prescribe silver. Apply the *Masnui* Logic. Ask yourself: Is the factory broken?

Let us look at three distinct Parables from the Ledger of the Sun.

Parable 1: The Parable of the Scorched Throne (Sun High, Jupiter Low)

- *The Passenger:* A Captain of Industry, a CEO, or a high-ranking politician.
- *The Asset:* He has immense Authority (Strong Sun). He commands armies of employees. He is wealthy. His word is law.
- *The Suffering:* He suffers from severe panic attacks. He cannot sleep without medication. He feels a constant, burning dread in his chest. He screams at his subordinates. He trusts no one.
- *The Failed Remedy:* He wears massive Pearls, drinks from silver goblets, and has pundits chant *Chandrashtama* mantras. The relief is fleeing. The fire returns.
- *The Diagnosis:* You look at his chart. The Sun is exalted in Aries (Authority). But Jupiter is debilitated in Capricorn or sitting in the house of an enemy (e.g., House 10 with no support).
- *The Flaw:* He has achieved Authority (Sun) but has discarded Ethics or Wisdom (Jupiter). Perhaps he has disrespected his elders to get to the top. Perhaps he thinks he is God, ignoring the natural laws (Jupiter). He has the Fire, but

no Air to cool it. He is suffocating in his own heat.

- *The Chemistry:* **Sun (High) + Jupiter (Zero) = Scorched Earth.** There is no water because the heat has evaporated it all. His "Moon" has boiled away.
- *The Cure:* He does not need a pearl. He needs a Guru. The remedy is behavioral: He must bow to a teacher. He must visit a temple (Jupiter's house) regularly and sweep the floor. He must start a breathing practice (Pranayama - Jupiter). By re-introducing Jupiter (Oxygen) to his system, he cools the Sun down, and the Moon (Peace) naturally condenses.

Parable 2: The Parable of the Wind-Blown Leaf (Jupiter High, Sun Low)

- *The Passenger:* A scholar, a writer, a spiritual seeker, or a perpetual student.
- *The Asset:* He is full of wisdom (Strong Jupiter). He speaks of high philosophy. He is kind. He understands the cosmos.
- *The Suffering:* He is constantly worried about survival. He has no money (Liquid Cash/Moon). He feels emotionally unmoored, drifting like a leaf in the wind. He is "too nice," and people trample him. He cannot pay his rent, yet he gives advice to the world.
- *The Diagnosis:* Jupiter is strong. But the Sun is weak or eclipsed. He has no spine. He has no boundaries. He cannot say "No."
- *The Flaw:* He has Wisdom (Jupiter) but lacks Discipline or Self-Respect (Sun). He allows others to dictate his life. He has the Air, but no Fire to give it direction.
- *The Chemistry:* **Jupiter (High) + Sun (Zero) = Cold Wind.** There is no "pot" to hold the water. His peace leaks out because he cannot say "No." His wisdom is useless because it has no vehicle.
- *The Cure:* He needs to establish boundaries. The remedy might involve strengthening the Sun: Waking up before sunrise, offering water to the Sun, or fixing his relationship

with his father. He needs to build the clay pot so that his wisdom can actually hold water. He must learn to be a King of his own life before he can be a Sage for others.

Parable 3: The Parable of the Poisoned Well (Both Corrupt)

- *The Passenger:* A man who appears pious and follows all rituals (Jupiter) but is secretly cruel to his family and arrogant about his status (Corrupt Sun). He uses religion as a weapon.
- *The Diagnosis:* The Moon here is completely artificial—it is a "Fake Moon." He projects peace, but inside is turmoil. He sleeps well only when he has destroyed an enemy.
- *The Chemistry:* **Corrupt Sun + Corrupt Jupiter = Poisoned Water.**
- *The Cure:* This is the hardest to cure. It requires a total dismantling of the ego (Sun). The remedy is service—cleaning the shoes of the devotees at the temple—to humble the Sun and purify the Jupiter.

3. The Technology of Gold: The Ultimate Remedy

One of the most famous, expensive, and cryptic remedies in the *Lal Kitab* for mental peace is: **"Wear Gold on the Body."**

Standard astrology says Gold is for Jupiter and Wealth. Why does the Red Book prescribe it for the Moon and Peace? Why does it not say "Wear Silver"?

The answer lies in the *Masnui* equation we have just decoded. This is not superstition; it is spiritual technology.

The Mechanics of the Circuit:

1. **Gold (The Conductor):** Gold is the metal of **Jupiter** (Wisdom/Ether). It is the most noble metal, resistant to corrosion, representing the purity of the Guru.
2. **The Body (The Ground):** The physical body, specifically the skeletal structure and vitality, is the domain of the **Sun**. The body is the "Chariot" of the soul.

3. **The Action:** When you place Gold (Jupiter) onto the physical Body (Sun)—whether as a chain around the neck or a ring on the finger—you physically enact the equation **Sun + Jupiter**. You are literally binding the element of Wisdom to the element of Self.
4. **The Result:** By bringing these two elements into permanent physical contact, you "manufacture" the **Moon** energy.

This acts as a continuous bio-feedback loop. Every time the gold touches the skin, it reinforces the union of Wisdom and Authority. It reminds the subconscious: *I am Authority (Sun), but I am guided by Wisdom (Jupiter).*

Historical Context: This explains why the ancient Rajas and Maharajas (Sun figures) were always draped in heavy gold jewelry (Jupiter). It was not merely a display of wealth. It was an alchemical necessity. A King sits on a throne of fire; he deals with war, execution, and judgment daily. To prevent himself from going mad or becoming a tyrant, he needed to be "cooled" constantly. The gold on his body manufactured the "Moon" energy, keeping his head cool and his heart peaceful amidst the chaos of the court. A King without gold is a King prone to madness.

Modern Application: For a person suffering from chronic anxiety or a "weak mind," wearing a gold chain or a gold ring is often more effective than wearing a moonstone.

- **The Moonstone** treats the symptom (the water). It cools the water temporarily.
- **The Gold** treats the source (the factory). It ensures the water is being produced correctly.
- *Note on Purity:* The *Lal Kitab* emphasizes that the gold must be yellow (Jupiter's color). White gold or platinum does not carry the Jupiter frequency in the same way. The karat must be high (22k or 24k) to ensure the Jupiter element is pure.

4. The Warning of the False Moon

Aruna: "Is it truly that simple, Surya? Can a piece of metal replace the need for meditation?"

Surya: "Do not be naive, Aruna. The metal is the anchor, but the ship must still sail. There is a danger here. We can create a 'False Moon.' If a man wears gold but continues to lie to his teachers (Jupiter) or dishonor his father (Sun), the gold will turn into a shackle. The equation works both ways. **Corrupt Sun + Corrupt Jupiter = Poisoned Moon.** If you wear the gold of a Guru but act like a thief, the resulting energy will not be peace; it will be a fog of delusion. You will feel calm only because you have become numb."

This brings us to the most critical realization of the *Lal Kitab*: **Remedies are not magic wands; they are amplifiers of intention.** If you wear the Gold (Jupiter) to trick the world, the Sun (Truth) will eventually burn you. But if you wear it as a pledge to Wisdom, the Moon will rise in your heart even on the darkest night.

Aruna's Realization

Aruna sat in silence for a long moment. The metaphor of the laboratory had shifted his understanding of the heavens. He looked at his own hands, imagining the planets not as distant stars, but as clay and water in his grasp.

Aruna: "I see now, O Light. We have been foolish. We have been trying to fill a leaking bucket by pouring more water (Silver/Moon remedies) into it. We pray for peace, we beg for money, thinking these are gifts to be received from the sky. But the solution was never the water. The solution was to repair the bucket (Sun) and ensure it was placed on stable ground (Jupiter). Peace is not a gift; it is an engineering feat."

Surya: "You are learning, Charioteer. Peace is not a gift from the sky; it is a byproduct of structural alignment. If you wish to calm the tides of the mind, do not yell at the ocean. The ocean will not listen. Strengthen the Shore (Sun) and calm the Wind (Jupiter). The Ocean will settle itself. This is the secret of the Molecular Moon. It is the first step in the Lunar Tide.

"But, Aruna, water is not the only thing that moves the soul. There is another fluid, thicker and sweeter than water, that drives men to madness and glory. We have learned how to create Peace (Moon). Now, we must learn how to create *Desire*. Turn the page, Charioteer. We must now look at the most dangerous equation in the book. We must enter the forge where **Venus** is made. And to do that, we must summon the Demons."

CHAPTER 2: THE STRUCTURE OF DESIRE

(The Alchemical Equation: Rahu + Ketu = Venus)

The Forge Of The Demons

We have spoken of Water (The Moon). We have learned that Peace is a manufactured product, created by the cooling of the Sun (Authority) by Jupiter (Wisdom). The formula was elegant. It was noble. It was the marriage of the King and the Priest. It makes sense to the mind that Goodness + Wisdom = Peace.

But life, Aruna, is not just about Peace. If men only wanted peace, they would all be monks living in caves, staring at blank walls. The Chariot does not just drive on flat, smooth roads. It drives through bazaars, through gardens, through festivals, and into the arms of lovers.

Men want Gold. Men want Luxury. Men want the intoxicating embrace of a wife. Men want Art, Beauty, Scent, and the sweet nectar of worldly success. They want the "Good Life." In the language of the *Lal Kitab*, this sweetness is called **Venus** (Shukra).

In standard astrology, Venus is the Goddess of Love, the planet of poetry and romance. She is soft, she is white, she is pure. We imagine her rising from the sea foam, untouched by the grime of the world. But in the *Lal Kitab*, Venus has a darker, more complex origin. She is not merely a gift from the heavens. She is a *synthetic element*. She is born of a collision between two monsters.

To understand Desire, we must enter the "Forbidden Laboratory." We must look at the second Great Equation of *Masnui Grah*. We must look at how the Universe manufactures "The Angel" out of the raw materials of Obsession (Rahu) and Destruction (Ketu).

The Dialogue: The Dragon's Synthesis

Aruna stood at the edge of the celestial Chariot, looking down at the swirling mists of the Earth. He saw the smoke of factories and the lights of the pleasure districts.

Aruna: "O Surya, I am uneasy. We are entering the domain of Shukra. The scriptures call him the *Daitya Guru*—the Teacher of the Demons. Yet, they also say Venus is the significator of the Wife, the Sperm, the Luxury Car, and the blooming flower. How can the same force be a Demon's Teacher and a Man's greatest joy? Why do I feel a shadow approaching the Chariot?"

Surya smiled, but it was not the warm smile of the morning; it was the knowing, twilight smile of the setting sun.

Surya: "Because, Charioteer, the flower grows from dirt. The lotus blooms from the mud. You asked me about the paradox of the King. Now, ask me about the paradox of the Lover. Have you not seen men who are brilliant thinkers—men who can imagine cities in the clouds—yet they die in poverty, their dreams unbuilt?"

Aruna: "I have. I see them in the coffee houses, sketching plans on napkins that eventually turn to trash."

Surya: "And have you not seen men who work harder than oxen, who carry the stones and till the fields until their backs break, yet they never taste the fruit of their labor? They build palaces for others but sleep in huts."

Aruna: "I have. They are the salt of the earth, yet they remain thirsty."

Surya: "Precisely. The Dreamer has the **Head** (Rahu). The Laborer has the **Feet** (Ketu). The Head can see the destination but cannot walk to it. The Feet can walk forever but do not know where they are going. Both are incomplete. Both are suffering. But... when the Head meets the Feet... when the Idea meets the Action... what is born?"

Aruna: "A result? A completed task?"

Surya: "More than a result. A *Satisfaction*. A Delight. A Creation. Write this in your ledger, Aruna, and write it in red ink, for it is the secret of all material success in the Kali Yuga: **Rahu + Ketu = Venus."**

Aruna recoiled. "This is impossible! Rahu is the North Node, the mouth that never closes, the smoke of illusion. Ketu is the South Node, the tail that cuts and detaches, the headless monk. They are the enemies of the Luminaries! They eclipse the Sun and Moon! How can two Malefics, two Demons, combine to create the most Benefic planet of all?"

Surya: "It is the greatest alchemy of the cosmos. It is the synthesis of the Dragon. **Rahu** is Ambition, Imagination, the 'I Want.' It is the Design. **Ketu** is Execution, Motion, the 'I Do.' It is the Construction. When the Ambition (Rahu) is grounded in Reality (Ketu), the result is **Venus**—the luxury that you can actually hold in your hand. Without Rahu, Venus is boring; it is just a plain white sheet. Without Ketu, Venus is a hallucination; it is a mirage of water in the desert. True Luxury is not magic, Charioteer. It is the perfect synchronization of the Shadow Head and the Shadow Tail. Venus is the *Sanjivani Vidya*—the power to bring the dead to life. And to bring life, one must master the forces of death."

The Decoding: The Mechanics Of Pleasure

This equation—**Rahu + Ketu = Venus**—is the "Theory of Manifestation" in the *Lal Kitab*. It is a radical departure from classical Vedic thought, which views the Nodes merely as karmic obstructions. The Red Book argues that without these two "demons," life would be devoid of flavor, progress, art, and reproduction.

- **Venus** is the *Karaka* (Significator) of the Wife, the Semen (Potency), Art, Currency, and the Skin.
- But Venus does not generate its own energy. In the *Masnui* system, it is the *fruit* of a tree where Rahu is the branches reaching for the sky, and Ketu is the roots digging into the earth.

1. The Ingredient Analysis

To fix a broken love life, a lack of luxury, or an inability to "enjoy" wealth, we must analyze the two demons that create the angel. We must enter the engine room of Desire.

Ingredient A: Rahu (The Architect / The Smoke) Rahu is the Head of the Dragon. In the context of Venus, it represents:

- **The Idea:** The blueprint, the scheme, the clever hack, the ambition to be great. It is the *Visualization*.
- **The Future:** Technology, electronics, the internet, the screen.
- **The Smoke:** Illusion, but also the "Cloud" that carries the rain. It is the mysterious allure—the "spark" in a romance.
- **In the Body:** The Brain's visual cortex, the Thoughts, the Phlegm.
- **The Flaw:** If Rahu is uncontrolled, it becomes obsession, paranoia, and greed. It becomes a hunger that cannot be sated.

Ingredient B: Ketu (The Builder / The Foundation) Ketu is the

Tail of the Dragon. In the context of Venus, it represents:

- **The Action:** The feet, the movement, the travel.
- **The Substance:** The physical bricks, the clay, the biological seed (sperm/ovum).
- **The Past/Roots:** Ancestry, the foundation, the son.
- **The Stability:** The ability to sit in one place (or move toward a goal) and *finish* the task.
- **In the Body:** The Feet, the Spine, the Ears, the Nerves.
- **The Flaw:** If Ketu is uncontrolled, it becomes detachment, destruction, amputation, and aimless wandering.

The Reaction: Venus (The Fruit) When the **Idea (Rahu)** is executed with **Stability (Ketu)**, the result is a tangible asset. That asset is Venus.

- Rahu (The Blueprint of the Palace) + Ketu (The Bricks and Mortar) = **Venus (The Palace).**
- Rahu (The Desire for a Child) + Ketu (The Biological Seed) = **Venus (The Birth/Family).**
- Rahu (The Screenplay) + Ketu (The Film Crew) = **Venus (The Movie).**

The Great Secret: If you want to increase your Wealth (Venus), you do not just pray to Goddess Lakshmi. You must check your Rahu and Ketu. Are you thinking big enough (Rahu)? And are you working hard enough (Ketu)? If one is missing, Venus cannot manifest.

2. The Diagnostic Parables

The *Lal Kitab* is best understood through the failures of men. When a Passenger comes to you complaining of "Bad Luck in Love," "Poverty," or "Fertility Issues," do not look at Venus alone. Look at the Nodes. The flaw lies in the mixture.

Parable 1: The Merchant of Smoke (High Rahu, Broken Ketu)

- *The Passenger:* An entrepreneur, an inventor, a startup founder, or a creative genius.

- *The Aura:* He is electric. He talks fast. He has a new idea every minute. He promises to change the world. He talks of millions.
- *The Reality:* He is broke. He lives in a messy, chaotic apartment. He borrows money to pay for coffee.
- *The Love Life:* He falls in love instantly (Rahu). He idealizes the woman, writing her poems, promising her the moon. But within two months, the relationship collapses. Why? Because he cannot handle the *reality* of a relationship—the grocery shopping, the bills, the boredom. He wants the fantasy, not the wife.
- *The Flaw:* **Rahu is High** (Excessive Thinking/Illusion), but **Ketu is Broken** (No Execution/No Feet).
- *The Alchemy:* **Smoke (Rahu) + No Earth (Ketu) = Fog.** There is no Venus here. There is only the *illusion* of Venus. He is a "Catfish" of destiny—presenting an image that has no substance.
- *The Fix:* We must strengthen Ketu. We must give him feet.
    - *The Behavioral Remedy:* Stop planning. Stop dreaming. Start walking. Literally. The remedy is to travel (Ketu). He must focus on his "Son" (if he has one) or keep a dog (Ketu). He must clean his house (Ketu represents the foundation). He must finish one small task before starting a new one.
    - *The Stone:* A Cat's Eye (Lehsunia) or wearing gold in the ears (to block the Rahu smoke from entering via the Ketu/Ears channel).

Parable 2: The Headless Mule (High Ketu, Broken Rahu)

- *The Passenger:* A factory worker, a mid-level manager, or a loyal servant.
- *The Aura:* He is quiet. He is tired. His hands are rough. He works 14 hours a day. He is honest to a fault.
- *The Reality:* He is exploited. He makes money for others, but stays poor himself. He has no savings.
- *The Love Life:* He is married, but there is no spark. The

marriage is functional, like a machine. His wife is unhappy because he is "boring" or "always working." There is no romance, no poetry, no *Rahu*.

- *The Flaw:* **Ketu is High** (Excessive Action/Drudgery), but **Rahu is Weak** (No Vision/Ambition).
- *The Alchemy:* **Motion (Ketu) + No Direction (Rahu) = Treadmill.** He is running on a treadmill. He is sweating, but going nowhere. He generates heat, but no light.
- *The Fix:* We must stimulate Rahu. We need to add some smoke to the fire.
    - *The Behavioral Remedy:* He needs a strategy. He needs to stop working with his hands and start working with his head. He needs to use technology (Rahu). He needs to clean the rust off his roof (Rahu). He needs to take his wife to a movie (Rahu activity) to reignite the Venus.
    - *The Risk:* If he only strengthens Ketu (e.g., by fasting), he will become an ascetic, and Venus will vanish entirely. He needs *Blue* energy (Rahu).

Parable 3: The War of the Nodes (The Broken Marriage)

- *The Passenger:* A couple on the verge of a violent divorce.
- *The Diagnosis:* The husband has High Rahu (Obsessive, suspicious, watching pornography, always looking outside for "more"). The wife has High Ketu (Detached, spiritual, cutting ties, refusing to communicate).
- *The Alchemy:* **Suspicion (Rahu) + Detachment (Ketu) = Explosion.** Venus cannot survive in this environment. The flower withers because the air is toxic (Rahu) and the roots are cut (Ketu).
- *The Tragedy:* They attract each other because they are opposites, but they destroy each other because they cannot synthesize.
- *The Fix:* They must find a "Third Element" to bind them. Often, in the *Lal Kitab*, the birth of a **Son** (Ketu) calms the Rahu of the father. Or, they must build a house (Saturn) to-

gether. They need a container for their energies.

3. The Dangerous Synthesis: Why Venus is a "Demon"

Aruna: "Surya, if Venus is the result of these two, why is it considered a Benefic? Is it not tainted by its parents? How can the Child of Smoke and the Headless Corpse be beautiful?"

Surya: "That is why Venus is the *Guru of the Asuras* (Demons). Do not forget this mythology. Jupiter is the *Deva Guru* (Teacher of Gods). Venus is the *Daitya Guru* (Teacher of Demons). Why? Because only Venus knows how to handle Rahu and Ketu. Only Venus has the *Sanjivani Mantra*—the secret of immortality. Think of it this way: Jupiter teaches you how to leave the world (Moksha). Venus teaches you how to *live* in the world (Bhoga). To live in the world, you must deal with desire, greed, lust, and matter. You must deal with demons. Venus takes the raw, dangerous energy of Rahu (Obsession) and refines it into **Passion**. Venus takes the raw, destructive energy of Ketu (Cutting) and refines it into **Sculpting**. But this makes Venus dangerous. If the mixture is wrong... if the alchemy fails... If Rahu dominates... Venus becomes **Lust, Adultery, and Addiction**. If Ketu dominates... Venus becomes **Perversion, Impotence, or Renunciation**. A pure Venus is rare. It requires a perfect balance of 'I want' (Rahu) and 'I surrender' (Ketu)."

4. The Remedial Logic: The Curd and the Cow

Now we understand the most famous—and often misunderstood—remedies for Venus in the *Lal Kitab*. These are not random rituals; they are chemical adjustments to the Rahu-Ketu balance.

Remedy A: The Service of the Cow (Gau Mata)

- **The Instruction:** Serve a Cow (Kamdhenu) to heal a broken Venus.
- **The Logic:**
    - The Cow is the living embodiment of **Venus**. She is the

earth, the milk, the sustainer.

  - But look at the Cow's biology. She has a tail (**Ketu**) that is constantly moving, swatting away flies (distractions). She has a mouth/head (**Rahu**) that is constantly grazing, taking in the raw earth.
  - The Cow takes the Grass (Mercury/Earth) into her Rahu-Mouth, digests it in her stomach, and uses her Ketu-Tail to keep herself clean.
  - The result of this biological process is **Milk** (Moon/ Liquid Venus).
  - By serving the Cow, you are interacting with a creature that has *perfectly synthesized* its Head and Tail. You are tuning your energy to her frequency.

Remedy B: The Clean Wife / Clean Clothes

- **The Instruction:** Respect your wife and wear clean, washed, ironed clothes. Apply perfume (Ittar).
- **The Logic:**
  - Dirty, wrinkled clothes represent **Rahu** (filth/stains) and **Malefic Ketu** (torn fabric/threads).
  - When you iron your clothes, you remove the wrinkles (confusion/Rahu) and align the fibers (Ketu).
  - Scent (Perfume) is the specific frequency of Venus. Bad odor is Rahu.
  - A man in dirty clothes cannot command respect (Sun) nor attract luxury (Venus).
  - **The Psychological Shift:** To "manufacture" Venus, you must physically resemble Venus. You cannot act like a beggar (Ketu) and expect the rewards of a King (Venus). By dressing well, you signal to your own subconscious (Rahu) that you are worthy of wealth.

Remedy C: The Wall of the House

- **The Instruction:** Maintain the plaster on the walls. Do not let paint peel or dampness seep in.
- **The Logic:**
  - The **Wall** structure is Saturn/Ketu.
  - The **Paint/Beauty** on the surface is Venus.
  - The **Peeling/Dampness/Mold** is Rahu (Fungus/ Decay).
  - If the walls are peeling, it means Rahu is eating the Venus. The home becomes ugly. The peace leaves.
  - Fixing the wall is not just home repair; it is planetary repair. It is re-establishing the boundary between the Demon (Decay) and the Goddess (Beauty).

Remedy D: The Curd and the Fire

- **The Instruction:** Throwing Blue Flowers or Blue items into the dirt/drain to calm Rahu, or burying white Sorghum (Jwar) to stabilize Venus.
- **The Logic:** These are specific separation techniques. If Rahu is choking Venus (e.g., a scandal or an affair destroying a marriage), we must "distract" Rahu. We give Rahu its own food (Blue/Coal) and bury it, so it stops eating the Venus.

The Secret Of The Clay Pot (A Visual Metaphor)

Surya: "Imagine, Aruna, a clay pot filled with sweet water."

Aruna: "I imagine it."

Surya: "The Clay is **Earth/Mercury**. The Shape of the Pot—its boundaries, its bottom—is **Ketu** (The container, the limitation). The Empty Space inside the pot—the capacity to hold—is **Rahu** (The void waiting to be filled). The Water inside is **Moon**. But the **Utility** of the pot... the fact that it holds water and quenches thirst... that usefulness, that *value*, is **Venus**. If the pot has no shape (Weak Ketu), the water spills. It is just mud. If the pot has no space inside (Weak Rahu), it is a solid brick. It holds nothing. Only when the Shape (Ketu) and Space (Rahu) are perfect, does the Value (Venus) exist."

The Warning Of The One-Sided Demon

We must conclude this chapter with a warning. In the modern world, we are living in the **Age of Rahu**. We have screens (Rahu) everywhere. We have unlimited desire (Rahu). We have artificial intelligence (Rahu). But our **Ketu**—our connection to the earth, our patience, our ability to sit still—is dying. This is why, despite having more luxury (Venus objects) than any King in history, modern man is starving for connection (True Venus). We have the Smoke, but we have lost the Fire. We have the Pornography (Rahu), but we have lost the Intimacy (Venus).

To restore the Lunar Tide, to bring back the sweetness of life, we must rebuild our Ketu. We must learn to walk again. We must learn to wait again. For Venus is not grabbed; she is cultivated.

Aruna's Second Realization

Aruna looked down at the world of men with new eyes. He saw the bustling markets, the theaters, the lovers in the park, and the lonely men in high towers.

Aruna: "I used to think Desire was a simple thing, Surya. I thought men desired because they were hungry. But now I see... Desire is a construct. It is a bridge. The man who builds a bridge needs the vision of the other side (Rahu) and the stones to build the arch (Ketu). If he has only vision, he falls into the river. If he has only stones, he builds a wall, not a bridge."

Surya: "Yes. And Venus is the Bridge. It is the only thing that connects the Ghost (Rahu) to the Corpse (Ketu) and makes them Human. But be warned, Charioteer. A bridge can lead to a palace, or it can lead to a dungeon. Venus is the beautiful face of the Dragon. Treat her with respect, or the Dragon will wake up.

"Now that we have understood the Mind (Moon) and the Desire (Venus), we must ask a more terrifying question: Even if a man has Peace and Desire... can he *see* where he is going? Is he blind? We must now discuss the **Eyes of the Chariot**. Saturn is Darkness. Sun is Light. But who is the Pupil? Turn the page, Aruna. We must discuss the **Blind Star**."

CHAPTER 3: THE EYES OF THE CHARIOT

(The Concept of Andha Grah & The Blind Star)

The Paradox Of The Blind Driver

We have spent the previous chapters building the magnificent machine. We have ignited the **Sun**—the roaring Engine of the Soul. We have cooled the radiator with the waters of the **Moon** —the Peace of Mind. We have constructed the bridge of **Venus**— the Desire that pulls us forward—using the raw, volatile materials of the Dragon (Rahu and Ketu).

The Chariot is now heavy, gold-plated, and moving at speed. The wheels of Justice (Saturn) are turning. The horses of Wisdom (Jupiter) are breathing rhythmically. But there is a fatal flaw in this design that we have not yet discussed. A flaw that brings Empires to their knees and turns Kings into beggars.

Imagine a Chariot with wheels of diamond and an engine of pure stellar fire. It is faster than sound. It is invincible in battle. But the Charioteer driving it is stone blind.

What is the value of Speed if the driver cannot see the cliff edge? What is the value of Authority if the King cannot see the traitor standing in his own shadow?

In the ancient, cryptic diagnostic manual of the *Lal Kitab*, there exists a terrifying classification known as the *Andha Teva* (The Blind Chart) or *Ratandh* (Night Blindness). This diagnosis does not care how many "Royal Combinations" (Raja Yogas) you possess. It does not matter if your Sun is exalted in Aries or your Jupiter is sitting on a throne of gold. If the Chart is "Blind," the planets lose their intelligence. They become like wild elephants in a dark room—powerful, panic-stricken, and destructive.

We often assume, in our rudimentary understanding of astrology, that the **Sun** represents vision. This is a dangerous half-truth. The Sun represents *Light*. But Light is useless without an *Eye* to receive it. And in the subtle, anatomical engineering of the Red Book, the **Eye**—the Pupil, the Lens, the delicate organ that interprets the world—is governed by **Venus.**

The Dialogue: The Light And The Lens

Aruna stood at the helm of the Chariot, his hands white-knuckled on the reins. The cosmic wind howled past them, but his eyes were squeezed shut against the blinding brilliance of the stars. He felt the heat of Surya behind him, intense and overwhelming.

Aruna: "O Surya, stop the Chariot! I am afraid."

Surya: "Afraid? You are the Charioteer of the Dawn. You drive the Sun itself. What is there to fear in the open sky?"

Aruna: "The Light... it is too much. It burns. I cannot see the path, O King. I am blinded by the very brilliance I carry. Surely, Vision is your domain? Do the scriptures not call You *Chakshu*—the Eye of the World? Why then do I feel like I am driving into a void?"

Surya's voice rumbled like thunder, but it carried a note of deep, instructional patience.

Surya: "You confuse the *Lamp* with the *Lens*, Aruna. This is the mistake of all novices. I am the *Illuminator*. I provide the photons. I reveal what is hidden in the dark. But I do not *see*. I only shine. Tell me, Charioteer, if you stand in a room flooded with My light—a room brighter than a thousand noons—but your eyelids are sewn shut... is the room dark or bright to you?"

Aruna: "To the room, it is bright. But to me... it is pitch black."

Surya: "Exactly. The 'Darkness' is not in the world; it is in the organ of perception. You need more than Light to drive destiny. You need a Receptor. **Saturn** is the Night—the background canvas. **I (The Sun)** am the Day—the ink that writes upon it. But **Venus**... Venus is the Pupil. Venus is the delicate, watery aperture that allows the light to enter the brain and form an image. If Venus is burnt, the Charioteer is blind. If Saturn is hostile, the Charioteer is driving in a fog. And if I am weak, the Charioteer has eyes, but he stands in a dungeon with no torch. Vision, my friend, is a trinity. It is a delicate optical equation: **Vision = The Source (Sun) + The Background (Saturn) + The Lens (Venus).**"

Aruna opened his eyes, squinting against the glare. "So a man can be a King... he can have a strong Sun... and still be blind?"

Surya: "The history of your Earth is littered with them. Look at the tyrants who burned their own cities. Look at the wealthy merchants who trusted thieves and lost everything. They had absolute Power (Sun). They had the Drive (Mars). But they could not *see* reality. They marched their empires into the abyss because their *Venus*—their ability to perceive value, love, and nuance—was destroyed. To drive destiny, Aruna, you do not just need Power. You need Perspective. And Perspective is the gift of the Goddess, not the God."

The Decoding: The Physics Of Sight

This chapter deals with the "Optics" of Destiny. In standard Vedic astrology, we look at the 2nd House (Right Eye) and 12th House (Left Eye) to judge physical eyesight. But the *Lal Kitab* goes much deeper. It analyzes the *functional mechanics* of how a human being perceives reality.

It posits that "Bad Luck" is often just "Bad Vision." You didn't see the opportunity, or you didn't see the trap.

1. The Trinity of Vision

To understand the Blind Chart, we must first understand the healthy eye.

A. The Sun (The Projector / The Flash) The Sun creates the reality. It highlights the truth. A strong Sun means the life path is illuminated. The obstacles are visible. The potholes are seen.

- *The Defect:* If the Sun is too strong (e.g., Exalted in Aries but afflicted), it becomes a "Blinding Glare." It washes out the details. The person sees only their own Ego. They become "Snow Blind."

B. Saturn (The Contrast / The Retina) This is a crucial and often misunderstood concept. You cannot see light without darkness. Imagine a cinema screen. If the screen is white, and you project white light onto it, you see nothing. You need a *black* background to see the movie. Saturn provides the "Background Black." It represents the Retina—the dark screen at the back of the eye that catches the image.

- *The Defect:* If Saturn is scattered or weak, the person suffers from "Glare Blindness." They are overwhelmed by possibilities. They cannot focus. They lack the cynicism required to see the truth.

C. Venus (The Pupil / The Lens) Venus is the *organic tissue* of the eye. It is the lens that focuses the image.

- *Metaphor:* Think of Venus as the "Art of Seeing." It represents "Worldly Vision"—the ability to judge the value of things, to read social cues, to see the beauty in a product, to notice the sadness in a wife's eyes.
- *The Defect:* If Venus is damaged (by the Sun or Moon), the lens is cracked. The person sees a distorted world. They mistake a snake for a rope.

2. The Diagnosis of the Blind Chart (*Andha Teva*)

The term *Andha Teva* is one of the most feared classifications in the Red Book. It implies that the native is operating without a navigation system. No matter how hard they work (Mars) or how authoritative they are (Sun), they will eventually crash because they cannot see the curve in the road.

There are three primary conditions that create a Blind Chart:

Condition A: The Collision of Noon and Midnight (The 10th vs. 4th Axis) The 10th House is the Throne of the Sun (Noon/Career). The 4th House is the Bed of the Moon (Midnight/Peace/Home). In the *Lal Kitab*, planets in the 10th House "look at" planets in the 4th House.

- *The Blindness:* If two enemies (e.g., Sun and Saturn, or Mars and Saturn) occupy the 10th House, they create a conflict. This conflict generates "Smoke." Because the 10th House looks at the 4th, this smoke fills the 4th House.
- *The Result:* The Home (4th) is filled with the smoke of the Work (10th). The native cannot see their own happiness. They destroy their family in pursuit of a career, only to realize too late that the career was hollow. They are "blind" to the cost of their ambition.

Condition B: The Combust Venus (The Burnt Lens) If Venus sits too close to the Sun (within a few degrees), standard astrology calls it "Combust" (*Ast*). The *Lal Kitab* uses a more violent metaphor: "The Glare of the King has blinded the Wife."

- *The Metaphor:* The King (Sun) is so arrogant, so dominant, and so full of "I am," that the Queen (Venus/Perspective) cannot speak. She covers her eyes.
- *The Result:* The native has a huge Ego (Sun) but zero Taste, zero Empathy, and zero ability to enjoy life (Venus). They buy expensive things but have no style. They demand love but do not know how to give it. They are emotionally blind.

Condition C: The Saturnine Fog If Saturn acts as a malefic in the 1st House (The Throne) or aspects the Sun negatively, it is like driving with a windshield covered in mud.

- *The Result:* The native interprets every innocent gesture as a threat. They "see" enemies where there are none. They are blinded by paranoia.

The Diagnostic Parables

The *Lal Kitab* is a book of stories. To understand Blindness, we must look at the lives of the Blind Charioteers.

Parable 1: The King Who Walked into a Ditch (High Sun, Burnt Venus)

- **The Passenger:** A powerful politician, a High Court Judge, or the patriarch of a massive industrial family.
- **The Aura:** When he walks into a room, people stand up. His voice is a boom of thunder. He is decisive. He is the Sun personified.
- **The Blindness:** Despite his power, his personal life is a wasteland. He makes terrible investments in "luxury" projects that fail. He trusts sycophants who flatter him (Sun loves flattery) but misses the loyal advisor who critiques him (Venus).
- **The Tragedy:** In his home, he bulldozes over his wife's feelings. He buys her diamonds (Stone) but denies her affection (Venus). He genuinely cannot "see" why she is unhappy. He thinks, "I provide everything (Sun), why is there darkness?"
- **The Crash:** Eventually, he signs a document he shouldn't have, simply because his ego told him he was invincible. He walks off a cliff because he refused to wear spectacles.
- **The Remedy:** He needs to dim the lights to save the lens.
    - *The Action:* He must bow to his wife (Venus). He must publicly honor women. He must donate *Curd* (Venus) in a temple. He must stop wearing bright Red (Sun) and start wearing Cream/White (Venus). He must let the Queen speak.

Parable 2: The Artist in the Dark (High Venus, Weak Sun)

- **The Passenger:** A brilliant painter, a designer, or a poet.

- **The Aura:** He is soft-spoken. He has impeccable taste. He sees colors others miss. His Venus (Eye) is perfect. He is a master of the Lens.
- **The Blindness:** No one knows him. He lives in a basement. He creates masterpieces that sit in the dark. He cannot sell his work. He is cheated by galleries.
- **The Logic:** He has the Lens (Venus), but he has no Lamp (Sun). The room is pitch black. His talent is invisible because there is no Authority, no "Spotlight" to reveal it.
- **The Tragedy:** He sees the beauty of the world, but the world does not see him.
- **The Remedy:** He needs a Torch.
    - *The Action:* He needs a Patron (Sun figure). He must perform *Surya Namaskar*. He must wear a Copper coin around his neck. He does not need more talent (Venus); he needs exposure (Sun). He must stop being "too humble."

Parable 3: The Night-Blind Driver (Malefic Saturn)

- **The Passenger:** A conspiracy theorist, a paranoid businessman, or a jealous husband.
- **The Blindness:** He sees things that aren't there. He interprets a smile as a sneer. He thinks his partners are stealing from him. He thinks his wife is unfaithful.
- **The Logic:** His windshield (Saturn) is covered in the mud of past karma. The light is coming in, but it is distorted by the dirt on the glass. He is hallucinating monsters in the shadows.
- **The Remedy:** Clean the windshield.
    - *The Action:* Feed the crows (Saturn). Donate oil or liquor to the poor (Saturn). *Surma* (Kajal) buried in the ground creates a "grounding" for this dark energy.

The Remedial Surgery: Curing The Blind Star

The *Lal Kitab* offers specific, often surgical remedies for "Blindness." These are not general prayers; they are optical corrections for the soul.

1. The "Surma" (Kajal) Remedy: grounding the Darkness

- **The Item:** *Surma* is black kohl, traditionally used to line the eyes. In the chemical language of the book, it represents **Saturn.**
- **The Ritual:** Burying *Surma* in the ground (earth) in a deserted place.
- **The Logic:** Why bury eye makeup?
    - If Saturn is blocking your vision (making you paranoid or unlucky), you take the essence of Saturn (Black Surma) and bury it.
    - You are physically removing the "Darkness" from your line of sight and grounding it into the Earth.
    - This clears the windshield. It stops the "Evil Eye" (Nazar) and the internal paranoia.

2. Feeding the Blind: The Ultimate Karmic Tax

- **The Ritual:** Feeding 10 blind people.
- **The Logic:** This is one of the most powerful and mystical remedies in the Red Book.
    - A Blind Person represents a human embodiment of **Saturn** (Darkness) and a damaged **Venus** (Eye).
    - When a "Blind Charioteer" (you) feeds a physically blind person, you are performing an act of sympathetic resonance.
    - You are paying a "tax" to the Universe for your own sight. You are saying, "I acknowledge the darkness, I serve it, so please do not force me to live in it."
    - This is often prescribed when a person feels "lost," "confused," or "directionless" despite having money. It buys a "Lantern" for the Chariot.

3. The White Cow and the Sun

- **The Ritual:** If the Sun has burnt Venus (Ego destroying Happiness), feed a White Cow.
- **The Logic:** The Cow is Venus (The Earthly Mother). By feeding her, you are resurrecting the burnt planet. You are telling the Universe, "I value the Lens as much as the Light." It cools the burning Sun.

The Warning Of The One-Eyed King

There is a final nuance, Aruna, which you must record. There is a difference between being **Blind** and being **One-Eyed** (*Kana*).

A Blind man knows he cannot see. He walks cautiously. He asks for help. He is often safe because of his caution. But the One-Eyed man... the man who sees only half the truth... he is dangerous. He has the **Sun** (Power) but lacks **Venus** (Love). He sees the Law, but not the Human. He has **Rahu** (Ambition) but lacks **Ketu** (Spirit). He sees the Profit, but not the Cost.

The *Lal Kitab* warns us: "It is better to be blind and led by a dog, than to be one-eyed and led by your own arrogance." The remedies of Book 2 are designed to open *both* eyes—the Eye of Authority (Sun) and the Eye of Compassion (Venus/Moon).

Aruna's Third Realization

Aruna closed his eyes for a long moment, letting the wind rush past his face. He felt the vibration of the chariot beneath his feet. He realized that for years, he had been looking *at* the road, but not *seeing* the journey.

Aruna: "I understand now, O Light. Power without Perception is a curse. A King who cannot see the tears of his subjects is not a King; he is a disaster waiting to happen. An Artist who cannot find the light is just a ghost in the shadows. And a Driver who refuses to clean his windshield will eventually mistake a cliff for a horizon."

Surya: "Yes. The Chariot requires three things to drive safely: The **Engine** (Sun) to move. The **Coolant** (Moon) to sustain. The **Eye** (Venus) to navigate. If any one of these is broken, the destination is never reached.

"We have now assembled the vital fluids and the organs of the Charioteer. We have the Blood (Moon), the Semen (Venus), and the Eye (Venus/Saturn). But the Chariot must drive *somewhere*. It cannot float in the void forever. It must enter the Cities of Time. It must enter the **Twelve Houses**. It is time to descend from the theory into the practice. It is time to look at how the Moon—the Mind—behaves when it enters the First House of Identity. Prepare yourself, Aruna. We are entering the **House of the Ascendant**."

PART II: THE HORSE'S PATH

(The Moon in the 12 Houses of Destiny)

CHAPTER 4: THE RISING TIDE

(The Moon in Houses 1, 2, and 3: The First Quadrant)

The Descent Of The River

The Chariot of the Sun tilted forward.

For the first part of our journey, we had remained in the high, abstract atmosphere of the 'Hidden Laboratory.' We had floated in the ether, discussing the chemistry of Artificial Planets and the theoretical equations of Peace. But theory, Aruna, is clean. Life is dirty.

Aruna loosened the reins as the wheels touched the jagged landscape of the Zodiac. The silence of the cosmos was replaced by the noise of human existence—the cry of a newborn, the clinking of gold coins, the whisper of siblings plotting in the dark, and the roar of the marketplace.

Aruna: "O Surya, the air here is thick. It smells of dust and milk. We have synthesized the Moon in the laboratory; we know that Peace is the child of Authority and Wisdom. But now, the 'Water of Peace' must be poured into the vessel of a human life. And human lives are not uniform. Some are cups of gold, some are cracked clay pots, and some are rusted sieves."

Surya: "Precisely, Charioteer. Water has no shape of its own. It takes the shape of the container. The Moon represents the **Mind**, the **Mother**, the **Liquid Cash**, and the **Peace** of the native. But the *quality* of this peace depends entirely on the **House** it occupies. In the **1st**, the Moon is a King trying to rule without a sword. In the **2nd**, she is a Goddess in a Golden Temple. In the **3rd**, she is a frightened child lost in a jungle of vines. This is **Part II: The Horse's Path**. We will track the Moon through the twelve cities of destiny. Tighten your grip, Aruna. We enter the **First Quadrant** —the realm of **Self and Establishment**. Here, the Moon learns to stand, to eat, and to speak. Here, the River begins its flow."

House 1: The Cooling King

(The Moon in Aries: The Paradox of the Velvet Throne)

The Architecture of the House The 1st House is the **Lagna** (The Ascendant). It is the sunrise. It is the Throne of the Horoscope. By the immutable cosmic law, this house belongs to **Mars** (Aries) and is the exalted seat of the **Sun**. It is a house of Fire, Red Blood, Iron, and Bone. It is the house of the "I Am."

When the Moon (Water/Softness) sits here, it creates a magnificent astrological contradiction. It is **"The Cooling King."** Imagine a ruler who sits on a throne of burning iron, but he does not carry a sword. He carries a vessel of cool water. He does not command his subjects through fear; he commands them through benevolence. He does not demand taxes; he offers sustenance.

The Dialogue: The Fire and the Water

Aruna: "This seems dangerous, O Light. Water sitting on a throne of Fire? The laws of physics are cruel here. Either the Moon will boil away into steam, leaving the native empty... or the Fire will be extinguished, leaving the King weak, cold, and ambitionless. Can a King rule with a soft heart?"

Surya: "It is a delicate balance, Aruna, but it is not impossible. If the Moon is strong, the native becomes a **Velvet Emperor**. He conquers his enemies not by cutting off their heads, but by feeding them until they are too full to fight. He rules with a heart so vast that his subjects would die for him. He is often the eldest son, or he takes on the burden of the eldest. He is the glue that holds the dynasty together. But you are right to fear the Steam. The 1st House is the house of **Identity**. If the Moon here is unsupported—if the 'Fire' underneath is too hot or too weak—the native becomes 'Too Soft.' He becomes a King made of Wax. When the heat of life rises, he melts. He cannot say 'No.'

He absorbs the sadness of the world. He becomes a daydreamer, drifting on the tides of his own emotions, unable to hold the heavy sword of decision. To save him, we must not remove the Water. We must *contain* it. We must remind him that he sits on a Throne of Mars."

The Parable of the Red-Clad Saint

- **The Passenger:** A man of gentle demeanor. He has a glowing, round face (Moon rules the face). He speaks in a whisper. He is beloved by his mother and treats all women as goddesses.
- **The Crisis:** Despite his goodness, his life is a series of unfinished projects. He starts a business with enthusiasm (Mars), but the moment a customer is rude to him (Emotional Hurt/Moon), he closes the shop. He lacks the "thick skin" required for the throne. He is wealthy, but directionless. His mind flickers like a candle in the wind.
- **The Diagnosis:** The "Water" (Moon) has dampened the "Mars" (1st House). The engine is flooded. The King is drowning in his own empathy.
- **The Remedy: The Red Anchor.** The *Lal Kitab* prescribes a paradoxical remedy here. Usually, to cool a house, we add Moon. But here, the Moon is the problem. To save the Moon, we must strengthen **Mars.**
    - o *The Ritual:* The native should keep a **Red Handkerchief** in his pocket, or wear red undergarments always.
    - o *The Alchemical Logic:* Red is the color of **Mars**. The 1st House is the property of Mars. By wearing Red on the body (1st House), the native honors the Landlord. But more importantly, the Red Energy acts as a **Copper Vessel**. Water without a vessel spills and evaporates. Water inside a Copper (Red) Vessel takes shape. It becomes useful. The Red Handkerchief gives the "Soft Moon" a "Hard Spine." It turns the "Wax King" into a "Warrior Poet." It allows him to be kind, but stops him from being weak.

The Warning of the Green Parrot There is a strict, non-negotiable prohibition for the Moon in the 1st House: **Avoid Green.**

- **The Physics:** Green is **Mercury**. Mercury is the bitter enemy of the Moon.
- If this native paints his house green, wears green clothes, or surrounds himself with broad-leaved green plants, he invites the "Enemy Spy" into the Throne Room.
- The result is **Nervous Anxiety**. The "Cooling King" begins to shake. His peace is shattered by overthinking and suspicion. The Moon in the 1st must stay away from the color of the Parrot.

House 2: The Shiva Lingam

(The Moon in Taurus: The Exalted Guest)

The Architecture of the Temple The 2nd House is **Vrishabha** (Taurus). It is the House of Wealth, Family, Speech, and the Eyes. Here, the Moon is **Exalted** (*Ucca*). Why is the Moon exalted in Earth? Because the 2nd House is the Garden. When Water (Moon) meets Earth (2nd), it creates **Life**. It creates Growth. It creates Agriculture. The *Lal Kitab* calls this placement **"The Shiva Lingam."** Just as Lord Shiva holds the Moon on his head and catches the River Ganga in his locks to prevent her from smashing the earth, the 2nd House holds the Moon in its highest dignity. It is the **Temple of the Soul**.

The Dialogue: The Flow of the Ganges

Aruna: "This must be the most blessed position in the zodiac, Surya. The Queen in her highest glory. The Mother in the House of Wealth. Surely this native drowns in gold?"

Surya: "He does not drown, Aruna; he *irrigates*. The Moon in the 2nd House creates a 'River of Wealth.' But listen closely to the physics of rivers. A river remains fresh only as long as it *flows.* If you dam a river, it becomes a swamp. It breeds mosquitoes and disease. The wealth of the 2nd House Moon is unique. It increases **only when it is shared**. The *Lal Kitab* says: 'The more he feeds others, the more his granary fills.' This is the house of the **Guest** (*Atithi*). For this native, the Guest is not a burden; the Guest is the delivery mechanism of God."

The Parable of the Open Door

- **The Passenger:** A simple householder. He is not a king, but his home always smells of cooking food. He has a habit of inviting people to eat—neighbors, travelers, stray dogs.
- **The Destiny:** He notices a strange pattern. On days when he hosts a dinner, he receives unexpected money the next morning. On days when he turns a beggar away, he loses his wallet.
- **The Flaw:** As he gets older, he listens to bad advice. "Save your money," people say. "Why feed strangers?" He becomes miserly. He tries to hoard the "Water." He builds a dam.
- **The Crash:** The moment he stops the flow, the water rots. His mother falls sick (Moon afflicted). His education (Moon/Jupiter connection) stops. His eyes (2nd House) become weak. The Shiva Lingam dries up.
- **The Shiva Connection:** The 2nd House is the seat of **Lord Shiva** in the *Lal Kitab* anatomy. The Moon is Shiva's ornament. If the native disrespects his guests, he is effectively removing the Moon from Shiva's head. The result is the opening of the Third Eye—destruction of wealth.

The Remedial Logic: Atithi Satkar (Service to the Guest)

To maintain the high tide of the 2nd House, the native must perform the liturgy of the River.

1. **Feeding the Guest:**
   - *The Prescription:* Never let a guest (or a worker/maid) leave your house without offering them food or

at least **Sweet Water**.

- *The Physics:* The Guest represents the **Flowing Moon**. The 2nd House is the **Temple**. By feeding the guest, you are performing the "Abhishekam" (Ritual Bath) of the Shiva Lingam. You are pouring water on the stone. The energy you release returns to you as Gold.

2. **The Silver Brick:**

- *The Prescription:* Bury a solid brick of silver in the foundation of the house.
- *The Physics:* Silver is **Moon**. The Foundation is **Earth**. By burying the Silver, you anchor the Exalted Moon permanently in the home. It ensures that the "River" has a permanent bed and does not change course during bad transits. It creates a magnetic field of peace.

3. **The Prohibition of Bells:**

- *The Warning:* Do not keep loud, clanging bells (*Ghanti*) in the prayer room.
- *The Logic:* The Moon is Silence. The 2nd House Moon is a "Mirror of Peace." Loud noise (Ketu/Mars) shatters the mirror. Worship should be silent or soft.

House 3: The Green Moon

(The Moon in Gemini: The Poisoned Lake)

The Architecture of the Jungle The 3rd House is **Mithun** (Gemini). It belongs to **Mercury**. It is the house of Siblings, Communication, Short Travels, and Courage (Mars). This is a hostile environment. **Mercury** is Green. **Moon** is White. In the alchemy of the *Lal Kitab*, **Mercury hates the Moon**. Why? Because Logic (Mercury) despises Emotion (Moon). Logic wants to dissect; Emotion wants to feel. Logic cuts; Emotion heals. When the Moon enters the 3rd House, it is called **"The Green Moon"** or **"The Moon in the Jungle."** It is like a beautiful, small lake surrounded by poisonous, creeper vines. The water looks inviting, but it is laced with anxiety.

The Dialogue: The War of Nerves

Aruna: "I fear for the Queen here, Surya. She is in the house of her enemy. Mercury is the Prince of Trickery. Will he not deceive the simple Mother?"

Surya: "He does not just deceive her, Aruna; he *corrodes* her. Moon in the 3rd is a placement of **Mental Anxiety**. The native's mind is always racing. Mercury (Nerves) attacks the Moon (Peace). The native suffers from hallucinations, phantom fears, and a deep, shaking insecurity. He has wealth (Moon), but he cannot enjoy it because he is always calculating (Mercury) the risks. He counts his coins while his dinner gets cold. His wealth fluctuates wildly. One day he is a prince; the next, a pauper. And the greatest tragedy? **The Siblings.** The 3rd House rules the younger brother and sister. Here, the younger sibling often becomes the enemy or a drain on the native's resources. The 'Arm' (3rd House) attacks the 'Heart' (Moon)."

The Parable of the Thirsty Traveler

- **The Passenger:** A writer, a salesman, or a media person (Mercury professions). He is brilliant, sharp-tongued, and neurotic.
- **The Crisis:** He makes a fortune in a trade deal, but loses it the next week in foolish speculations. He trusts people who flatter him (Mercury's trick), only to be betrayed. He feels a constant dryness in his throat—a physical manifestation of the Moon drying up in the Wind (Air sign).
- **The Conflict:** He tries to use logic to solve emotional problems. He analyzes his love life with a calculator. He creates spreadsheets for his relationships. This kills the joy. The Lake becomes a swamp of data.
- **The Destiny of the Daughter:** The *Lal Kitab* warns that the native's daughter (Mercury) represents the 3rd House. Her birth often coincides with a fluctuation in wealth—either

a massive gain or a massive loss, depending on the Moon's aspect.

The Remedial Logic: The Sweet Water (Sherbat)

To save the Green Moon, we must introduce a third element that can defeat Mercury and support the Moon. That element is **Mars** (The Courage/The Landlord of the 3rd House's energy). But we cannot use "Fire Mars" (Red); that would boil the small lake. We need "Sweet Mars."

1. **The Sweet Water Ritual:**
   - *The Prescription:* Offer **Sweet Water** (Sherbat) or Jaggery-Water to thirsty people in the summer.
   - *The Alchemical Physics:*
     - Water is **Moon.**
     - Sugar/Jaggery is **Mars.**
     - When you mix them, you create **Chandra-Mangal Yoga** (The Moon-Mars Wealth Combination).
     - Mars is the only planet that can control Mercury. Mercury fears Mars.
     - By mixing Sugar (Mars) into Water (Moon), you create a weapon that Mercury fears. You turn the "Poisoned Water" into "Nectar." You arm the Moon with the sweetness of Mars.
2. **Serve the Kanya (Girl Child):**
   - *The Prescription:* Bow to young girls (Kanyas) and give them gifts or sweets.
   - *The Physics:* Young girls are the living avatars of **Mercury**. By serving them, you appease the Enemy Landlord. You turn the "Trickster Spy" into a "Friend." You make a treaty with the jungle.
3. **The Silver Ring:**
   - *The Prescription:* Wear a plain silver ring.
   - *The Physics:* This strengthens the Moon directly. It acts as a shield against the corrosive green fog of Mercury. It reminds the native to feel, not just think.

Summary Of The Rising Tide

Aruna looked back at the first three cities. He saw the Red King, the Exalted Guest, and the Poisoned Lake.

Aruna: "The Path is treacherous, Surya. In the **1st**, the Moon needed the **Red of Mars** to find its spine. In the **2nd**, the Moon needed the **Guest** to unlock its vault. In the **3rd**, the Moon needed the **Sweetness of Mars** to survive the poison of Mercury."

Surya: "You are learning the Grammar, Charioteer. Peace is not a passive state. It is an active engineering of forces. You cannot just 'be' peaceful. You must build a structure that *allows* peace to exist. But the Chariot moves on. The Moon must now leave the Jungle of the 3rd House. It must enter the **Domestic Quadrant**. It flows into the **River of the Mother (4th)**. It enters the **Desert of the Future (5th)**. And it descends into the **Well of the Underworld (6th)**. Prepare yourself. The specific laws of Milk and Water are about to change. We are about to learn why selling milk can destroy a dynasty. Turn the page to **Chapter 5**."

CHAPTER 5: THE DOMESTIC TIDE

(The Moon in Houses 4, 5, and 6: The Second Quadrant)

The Departure From The Jungle

Aruna pulled the reins, his hands trembling slightly from the strain. The Chariot had just navigated the tangled, vine-choked forests of the 3rd House—the domain of the "Green Moon." The air there had been suffocating, filled with the noise of anxiety, the whispers of siblings, and the corrosive green fog of Mercury. It was a place where peace had to be fought for with a sword.

But now, as the celestial wheels turned forward, the landscape opened up.

The dense canopy of trees receded. The ground leveled out. Ahead of the Chariot lay a view that stole the breath from the Charioteer's lungs. It was a vast, shimmering expanse of water —a river so wide it looked like the sea, flowing gently under the light of a silvery, full moon. The air was cool, smelling of wet earth and night-blooming jasmine.

Aruna: "O Surya, the noise has stopped. The green fog is gone. I see no enemies, no traps, no poison. The water here is clear and deep. This feels... safe. This feels like a homecoming."

Surya: "It is a homecoming, Aruna. We have left the **First Quadrant** of Self-Establishment. We are entering the **Second Quadrant**—the **Domestic Tide**. Here, the Moon is no longer fighting to exist. Here, the Moon rules. In the **4th House**, the Moon is the **Queen in her own Palace**. In the **5th**, she becomes the **Water in the Desert**. In the **6th**, she descends into the **Well of the Underworld**. This is the heart of the chart. This is where the private life of the native is written. But beware, Charioteer. The danger in the Jungle (3rd) was obvious—a tiger shows its teeth. The danger in the River (4th) is subtle. A man can drown in the most beautiful water if he does not know how to swim. And the danger in the Desert (5th) is evaporation—if you do not cover the pot, the sun steals your soul. Let us navigate the **River of Plenty**."

House 4: The River Of Plenty

(The Moon in Cancer: The Infinite Spring)

The Architecture of the Palace The 4th House is **Kark** (Cancer). It is the natural zodiac sign of the Moon. It represents the **Mother**, the **Chest/Heart**, the **Vehicle**, the **Home**, the **Ancestral Property**, and the ultimate **Peace of Mind**. When the Moon sits here, she is sitting on her own throne. She is powerful, benevolent, and infinite. The *Lal Kitab* calls this placement **"The High Tide"** or **"The River of Plenty."** Unlike the 2nd House (where wealth comes from guests), the 4th House wealth comes from the **Source**. The native *is* the Source.

The Dialogue: The Dam and the Flood

Aruna: "This seems perfect, O Light. The Planet of Peace in the House of Peace. Surely this native has no worries? Surely his coffers are always full?"

Surya: "His coffers are not just full, Aruna; they are *refilling*. The Moon in the 4th House operates on a unique law of physics: **Expense is the Fuel of Income.** Listen closely, for this contradicts the economics of men. For most men, spending money reduces their wealth. For the Moon in 4th native, spending money *increases* it. The River must flow. As long as he gives, the mountain sends more water. If he builds a dam—if he tries to hoard, to be miserly, to stop the expense—the River backs up. It floods the villages upstream (the Ancestors) and dries up the villages downstream (the Children)."

Aruna: "So he must be a Spendthrift to be a King?"

Surya: "He must be a **Conduit**. But there is one specific, fatal trap here. A trap so simple that millions fall into it."

Aruna: "What trap can hide in such clear water?"

Surya: "The Sale of the Mother. Milk is the essence of the Moon. The 4th House is the Mother. If this native decides to become a merchant of milk—if he opens a dairy, or sells water for profit—he commits a spiritual crime. He turns the 'Mother' into a 'Prostitute.' He sells the very essence of his protection. The moment the first coin is exchanged for milk, the River turns to poison. The family line halts. The mind shatters."

The Parable of the Landlord's Ruin

- **The Passenger:** A wealthy landlord born with a silver spoon. He owns land, horses, and a massive ancestral home (4th House domains). He is the pillar of his community. His mother is alive and healthy, and his house is always full of relatives.
- **The Temptation:** He sees that he has 50 cows on his estate. He thinks, "Why am I giving this milk away to the villagers for free? I am a businessman. I should start a dairy empire. I will become the Milk King."
- **The Violation:** He builds a factory. He starts selling milk to the city. He puts a price tag on the White Fluid.
- **The Collapse:** Within two years, the tragedy strikes. His eldest son (5th House) develops a mysterious mental disorder—he stops speaking (Moon affliction). His wife (Venus) is diagnosed with a fluid-related illness (dropsy or blood infection). His gold is stolen by his own servants.
- **The Diagnosis:** The "River" has turned against him because he tried to commercialize the Goddess. He built a dam of greed, and the dam burst.
- **The Burn:** The *Lal Kitab* specifically warns that if "Milk boils over and falls into the fire" frequently in this house, it is an omen of doom. It signifies the Moon being scorched by Mars.

The Remedial Logic: The Free Flow

To maintain the Infinite Spring, the native must respect the sanctity of the Source.

1. **The Prohibition of Selling Milk:**
   - *The Law:* Never, under any circumstances, trade in milk, water, or white liquid products.
   - *The Logic:* You can give milk freely. You can make sweets (*Kheer*) and give them away. But you cannot take money for the white fluid. It breaks the "Mother-Child" bond and replaces it with a "Merchant-Customer" bond. If you sell the Mother, who will protect you?
2. **The Public Water Dispenser (Pyaau):**
   - *The Prescription:* Set up free water dispensers in public places, especially during summer.
   - *The Alchemical Physics:* By letting water flow freely to the thirsty (especially the poor/Saturn), you physically enact the "River" archetype. You tell the Universe: "I am the Source. I give freely." The Universe responds by ensuring the Source never runs dry. The more water flows out, the more gold flows in.
3. **The Mother's Health:**
   - *The Secret:* The health of the mother is the **Financial Barometer** of this native.
   - If the mother is sick, the bank balance drops. If the mother is happy, the wealth rises.
   - *The Remedy:* Touching the mother's feet and serving her is not just duty; it is the most powerful "Investment Strategy" for a Moon in 4th native.

House 5: Water In The Desert

(The Moon in Leo: The Secret Spring)

The Architecture of the Desert The 5th House is **Simha** (Leo). It belongs to the **Sun**. It is the House of the King, the Divine Intellect, the Progeny, and the Future. Geographically, the 5th House is a dry, hot, expansive landscape. It is a **Desert**. When the Moon enters here, it is **"Water in the Desert."** It is a precious resource. It is life-saving. The Moon here represents the **"Truthful Mouth"** and the **"Cool Mind of the Advisor."** But water in a desert has one great enemy: **Evaporation**.

The Dialogue: The Vapor of Words

Aruna: "The heat here is intense, Surya. The River of the 4th House has disappeared. I see only a small oasis in the middle of burning sands. Will the Moon survive the Sun's glare?"

Surya: "She survives only if she is *covered*, Aruna. In the 5th House, the Moon becomes a secret treasure. If the native exposes his emotions, his plans, or his wealth to the world, the Sun burns them away. The *Lal Kitab* calls this the house of **'Parda'** (The Veil). This native must be a man of secrets. If he shouts his plans from the rooftop, they will fail. If he weeps in public, he loses his dignity. But if he keeps his water in a covered pot... ah, then he becomes the **Advisor to Kings**."

Aruna: "Why Advisor? Why not King?"

Surya: "Because the King is the Sun. The Advisor is the Cool Mind (Moon) behind the King. The Moon in the 5th gives the native **Vak Siddhi** (The Power of Truthful Speech). Because water is scarce here, every drop counts. Every word he speaks carries the weight of destiny."

The Parable of the Loose-Tongued Prophet

- **The Passenger:** A man of high intellect and intuition. He works as a consultant or a strategist. He often guesses the outcome of events before they happen.
- **The Flaw:** He loves to talk. He tells his friends about his business ideas before the contract is signed. He boasts about his children's success at parties. He reveals his own

weaknesses to strangers, thinking he is being "honest."

- **The Evaporation:** Every time he speaks of a "Sure Thing," it fails. The deal collapses at the last minute. His children (5th House), whom he brags about, start to fail in school or turn against him.
- **The Diagnosis:** He has exposed the Water to the Sun. The steam has escaped. By lifting the lid (Secrecy), he allowed the pressure (Shakti) to dissipate.
- **The Crisis of Greed:** The 5th House is also the **House of Speculation** (Lottery/Stocks). If this native tries to use his intuition for gambling or "easy money," the Moon turns to acid. The *Lal Kitab* warns: **"If he becomes greedy, his own semen (Progeny) is destroyed."**

The Remedial Logic: The White Flag

To protect the Water from the Sun, we must use the symbol of the Moon as a shield.

1. **The White Handkerchief:**
   - *The Prescription:* The native must *always* keep a clean **White Handkerchief** in his pocket (preferably the front pocket or near the heart).
   - *The Alchemical Physics:* White is the color of the **Moon.** The Pocket (near the stomach/thigh) represents the **5th House** area in the body's geography. By keeping the "White Flag" close to the body, you create a "Cloud" that shades the desert. You signal to the Universe that the Moon is present and protected. It cools the arrogance of the Sun.
2. **The Law of Secrecy (Parda):**
   - *The Prescription:* "Do not reveal the pregnancy of the wife, the profit of the business, or the pain of the heart until the cycle is complete."
   - *The Physics:* Secrecy acts as a **Lid** on the pot. It prevents the energy from evaporating. For this native, silence is not just golden; it is survival.

3. **Service on the Mountain:**
   - *The Prescription:* Walk on mountains or visit hill stations.
   - *The Physics:* Mountains are the **Sun/Jupiter**. The Moon rises higher in the mountains. This elevates the native's thinking from "Greed" to "Wisdom."

House 6: The Water Of The Underworld

(The Moon in Virgo: The Deep Well)

The Architecture of the Abyss The 6th House is **Kanya** (Virgo). It belongs to **Mercury** (The Enemy) and **Ketu** (The Eclipse). It is the House of Sickness, Debt, Litigation, Enemies, and the **Underworld** (*Patal*). When the Moon falls here, it is **"The Moon in the Deep Well."** The water is there, but it is far below the surface. It is dark, stagnant, and hard to reach. The Sun's light does not reach the bottom of a deep well. This is the placement of **Psychosomatic Illness, Depression**, and **Hidden Sorrows.**

The Dialogue: The Stagnant Pool

Aruna: "I shudder to look down, O Light. The well is deep and mossy. I see a reflection at the bottom, but it is dim. Is the Moon dead here?"

Surya: "She is not dead, Aruna, but she is **Trapped**. Here, the Mind (Moon) is surrounded by Logic (Mercury) and Detachment (Ketu). The native overthinks. He dissects his own happiness until it bleeds. He feels a constant sense of doom, as if he is falling into a pit. He helps others—he gives water to the world—but the world gives him poison in return. This is the house of the **Healer**. But a Healer often absorbs the sickness of his patients."

Aruna: "Why does he suffer so?"

Surya: "Because he has opened a connection to the Underworld.

The danger here is **Suicide of the Mind**—giving up hope because the sky seems too far away. And the greatest mistake he can make is to physically manifest this 'Hole' in his own home."

The Parable of the Thirsty Nurse

- **The Passenger:** A person who works in service—a nurse, a social worker, or simply the "problem solver" of the family. He is the one everyone calls in an emergency.
- **The Crisis:** People come to him only when they are in trouble (6th House). He absorbs their trauma. He gives money to friends who never return it.
- **The Mother:** His mother is often visually impaired or chronically ill. The "Source" is broken.
- **The Mistake:** He decides to "improve the Vastu" of his house by digging a borewell, installing a sunken fountain, or building an underground tank in the center of the house.
    - *The Crash:* The moment the drill hits the water, his finances collapse. His mental health shatters.
    - *The Physics:* Digging a hole in the earth physically manifests the "Deep Well" of the 6th House. It gives the Moon a place to sink further. He has invited the Underworld into his living room.

The Remedial Logic: The Water of the Dead

To cure the Moon in the 6th, we must pay the debt of the Underworld. We cannot fight the darkness; we must serve it.

1. **Serving Water at the Cremation Ground:**
    - *The Prescription:* The native should arrange for water (buckets/pitchers) at a **Cremation Ground** (*Shamshan*) or a **Cemetery**. Alternatively, serve water to patients in a **Hospital**.
    - *The Alchemical Physics:* The Cremation Ground and Hospital are the physical locations of the **6th and 8th Houses** (Sickness/Death). Water is the **Moon**. By voluntarily taking the Moon (Water) to these places and

serving the grieving or the sick, you are **Paying the Rent**. You are telling the Lords of Death and Disease: "I am serving you voluntarily. I am bringing water to your domain. Do not come to my house to fetch it." This is the principle of **Voluntary Sacrifice**. If you serve the hospital, you don't have to be a patient in it. You vaccinate your destiny.

2. **The Prohibition of Milk at Night:**
   - *The Law:* **Never drink milk after sunset.**
   - *The Physics:* Night is **Saturn**. The 6th House is the house of "Cold Obstacles." Milk is **Moon**. Drinking milk at night in this placement turns the Moon into **Poison** (*Zahar*). It creates chronic cough, allergies, and depressive thoughts. The body cannot digest the Moon energy in the dark. *Correction:* Drink milk in the day (Sun's time), or drink Curd/Buttermilk (Venus) instead.
3. **The Rabbit Feed:**
   - *The Prescription:* Feed Rabbits.
   - *The Physics:* Rabbits are **Ketu**. In the 6th House, Ketu is the "Biting Dog" or the "Ghost." By feeding the rabbit, you appease the Eclipse factor. You turn the "Ghost" into a "Pet." You stop the drain on the mind.

Summary Of The Domestic Tide

Aruna wiped the mist from his face. They had traversed the River, the Desert, and the Well.

Aruna: "The Moon is resilient, Surya. In the **4th**, she is a Queen—but she must not become a Merchant. In the **5th**, she is a Prophet—but she must wear a Veil. In the **6th**, she is a Healer—but she must serve the Dead to stay alive."

Surya: "You see the pattern, Charioteer. The Moon takes the color of the earth she flows over. But the journey is only half done. We have dealt with the **Self** (Quadrant 1) and the **Domestic** (Quadrant 2). Now, the Chariot must climb the steep slope of the **Partnership Quadrant**. The Moon must face the **Merchant of the 7th**. She must descend into the **Grave of the 8th**. And she must climb the **Mountain of the 9th**. Prepare yourself, Aruna. The next chapter deals with the **Waning Tide**. We will see what happens when the Mother meets the Wife, and when the Mind meets Death. Turn the page to **Chapter 6**."

CHAPTER 6: THE WANING TIDE

(The Moon in Houses 7, 8, and 9: The Third Quadrant)

The Departure From The Well

The Chariot lurches upward.

Aruna wiped the cold dampness of the 6th House from his brow. For the last leg of the journey, the horses had struggled through the mud of the "Deep Well." They had navigated the stagnant waters of the Underworld, where the Moon served as a Healer in the house of Sickness. The air had been heavy with the smell of medicine and decay.

But now, the wheels struck stone pavement. The silence of the Well was shattered by the roar of a thousand voices.

The landscape transformed violently. The dark, enclosed walls of the 6th House fell away, revealing a sprawling, chaotic, and vibrant city. The smell of incense and wet earth was replaced by the scent of expensive perfume, roasting spices, and human sweat. Aruna saw merchants shouting prices, couples arguing in the streets, beggars pleading for coins, and pilgrims walking toward distant temples.

Aruna: "O Surya, the isolation is over. The Queen has left the nursery and the hospital. She is out in the open. But she looks... smaller here. In the 4th House, she was a giant River. Here, she is just a woman walking through a crowd."

Surya: "We have entered the **Third Quadrant**, Aruna. This is the **Waning Tide**. In the sky, the Moon wanes as it approaches the Sun. In the chart, the Moon 'wanes' in its softness as it approaches the harsh realities of the world. Here, the Mother must leave the protection of the Home and enter the **Bazaar of the 7th**. She must descend into the **Grave of the 8th**. And finally, she must rise to become the **Great Lake of the 9th**. This is the quadrant of **Interaction**. In the 7th, the Moon meets her Rival (Venus). In the 8th, she meets her Executioner (Death). In the 9th, she meets her God (Jupiter). Tighten the reins, Charioteer.

The Marketplace is more dangerous than the Jungle. In the Jungle, a tiger kills you to eat. In the Marketplace, a man kills you for profit."

House 7: The Merchant Of Emotion

(The Moon in Libra: The War of Milk and Curd)

The Architecture of the Bazaar The 7th House is **Tula** (Libra). It is the scales of the Zodiac. It belongs to **Venus** (The Wife/Luxury) and **Mercury** (Trade/Business). It is the House of **Marriage**, **Partnership**, and **Daily Business**. When the Moon enters here, it is an invasion. The Moon represents **Milk** (Mother/Pure Emotion). Venus represents **Curd** (Wife/Processed Desire). Astrologically, the 7th House is the home of Venus. When the Moon enters, it creates the **"Lakshmi-Narayan War."** It is the archetypal conflict between the Mother-in-Law and the Daughter-in-Law.

The Dialogue: The Curdling of the Soul

Aruna: "I see the conflict, O Light. Two Queens in one palace. One brings nourishment (Moon), the other brings pleasure (Venus). Can they not coexist? Does the Chariot not need both?"

Surya: "They can coexist only if they are kept in separate vessels, Aruna. If you mix Milk (Moon) and Curd (Venus), what happens? The Milk sours. It splits. It becomes useless. The Native with Moon in the 7th House faces this exact tragedy. If he brings his 'Mother' (Emotion) into his 'Business' (7th House), he gets cheated. If he brings his 'Mother' into his 'Bedroom' (Marriage), his wife rebels. This native is a **Merchant of Emotion**. He tries to trade in feelings. He uses liquid cash (Moon) to buy love (Venus). But the *Lal Kitab* warns: **'He who sells Milk and Curd together will lose his gold.'**"

The Parable of the Merchant Who Sold His Soul

- **The Passenger:** A charming, soft-spoken businessman. He deals in liquids, education, or textiles. He is the favorite son of his mother. He has a "Moon-like" face—round and pale.
- **The Marriage:** He marries a beautiful woman (Venus). Immediately, the war begins. His mother falls sick, or his wife refuses to live in the ancestral home. The peace (Moon) of the house evaporates. Every night is an argument.
- **The Business Error:** He enters a partnership. Because he has a "Moon Mind" (Soft), he trusts his partner like a brother. He signs contracts based on faith, not logic.
- **The Crash:** The partner cheats him. At the same time, his wife demands a divorce. The "Milk" has curdled. The *Lal Kitab* says: "His wealth fluctuates like the tide—High Tide in the morning, Low Tide at night." He is rich on Monday and poor on Friday.

The Remedial Logic: The Balance of Fluids

To save the Moon in the 7th, we must perform a chemical separation. We must distinguish between the Mother and the Wife.

1. **The Weighing of the Bride (Tula Daan):**
    - *The Prescription:* At the time of marriage (or as a remedy later), weigh the bride against **Rice and Milk**. Donate this weight in items to a temple or the poor.
    - *The Alchemical Physics:* The Bride is **Venus**. Rice and Milk are **Moon**. By weighing them against each other and then *giving the Moon away*, you are paying the "Moon Tax." You are telling the Universe: "I have paid the debt of the Mother (Moon). Now, let the Wife (Venus) enter the house without conflict." This ritual physically separates the two energies, preventing the "Curdling." It satisfies the Moon so she does not attack the Venus.
2. **The Prohibition of Water Trade:**
    - *The Law:* The native must **never** sell milk or water for profit in partnership.

- o *The Logic:* The 7th House is "Partnership." Moon is "Water." If you make Water the subject of Partnership, it will dry up. He can trade in dry goods (Saturn/Mercury), but not liquids.

3. **The Gold and Copper Shield:**

- o *The Prescription:* The native should wear Gold (Jupiter) and Copper (Sun).
- o *The Physics:* Jupiter and Sun are the "Elders." When the King (Sun) and the Guru (Jupiter) are present, the two fighting Queens (Moon and Venus) maintain their dignity. The Gold creates a buffer zone between the Milk and the Curd.

House 8: The Moon In The Grave

(The Moon in Scorpio: The Black Water)

The Architecture of the Smashan The 8th House is **Vrishchik** (Scorpio). It belongs to **Mars** (Death) and **Saturn** (Longevity). It is the **Cremation Ground** (*Smashan*). It is the house of Legacy, Sudden Events, and the Occult. Here, the Moon is **Debilitated** (*Neecha*). It is **"The Moon in the Grave."** It is not the fresh river of the 4th, nor the stagnant well of the 6th. It is **"Black Water"**—water that has touched death. Water that has been used to wash a corpse.

The Dialogue: The Ghost in the Machine

Aruna: "The air here smells of ash, Surya. The water is dark and oily. Surely the Moon dies here? How can Peace exist in the house of Death?"

Surya: "The Moon does not die, Aruna. Energy cannot be destroyed. But it becomes a **Ghost**. The native with Moon in the 8th is a soul who walks between worlds. He sees things others do not see. He has powerful intuition, but it is the intuition of disaster. He smells the rain before the cloud appears. But the tragedy is his **Fear**. Because his Mind (Moon) is sitting in the House of Death (8th), he is constantly afraid of dying. He suffers from **Depression**, **Paranoia**, and **Legacy Trauma**. He inherits the tears of his mother. The *Lal Kitab* says: 'The Moon in the 8th eats the maternal happiness.' His mother is either distant, sick, or suffers greatly during his birth."

The Parable of the Prince of Shadows

- **The Passenger:** A man who inherits a large legacy (8th House rules Wills). He does not work for his money. He lives in a large, dark house.
- **The Mind:** He is prone to severe mood swings. One moment he is ecstatic; the next he is planning his own funeral. He is drawn to the occult, to Tantra, and to dark secrets. He keeps secrets even from himself.
- **The Danger: Water Accidents.** The *Lal Kitab* warns: "Do not swim in deep rivers." The 8th House is the "Abyss." If the Moon native enters the water, the Abyss calls to him. He is prone to drowning or food poisoning (liquid poison).
- **The Gamble:** He tries to use his intuition for gambling (Lottery is 8th House). He wins once, then loses everything. The "Ghost" tricks him.

The Remedial Logic: The Vaccination of Death

The remedy for the 8th House is one of the most paradoxical and terrifying secrets of the *Lal Kitab*. To cure the fear of death, you must bring "Death" into your home.

1. **The Cremation Water Ritual:**
    - *The Prescription:* Bring water from a tap inside a **Cremation Ground** (*Shamshan Ghat*) or from a holy river where ashes are immersed (like the Ganges at Haridwar). Keep this water in a glass bottle in the house (store it high up, out of reach).
    - *The Alchemical Physics:* This acts on the principle

of **Homeopathic Vaccination**. The Native's mind is already trapped in the 8th House (Crematorium). Subconsciously, he is living in a graveyard. By physically bringing the "Water of the Crematorium" into his safe space and *containing* it (in glass), he "vaccinates" his home against the 8th House energy. He tells the Universe: "I already have the symbol of death here; you do not need to send the real thing." It satisfies the hunger of the 8th House. It turns the "Ghost" into a "Guardian."

2. **The Silver Square:**
   - *The Prescription:* Bury a **Square Piece of Silver** under the threshold (*Chaukhat*) of the house.
   - *The Physics:* **Silver** is Moon. **Square** is the shape of **Mars**. The Moon is weak in the 8th. Mars is the Landlord. By forcing the Moon into a Square shape, you give the Liquid a "Brick Structure." You arm the Moon with the weapon of Mars. Burying it at the threshold stops the "Death Energy" from entering the sanctuary.
3. **The Gram Pulse Offering:**
   - *The Prescription:* Donate 800 grams of Gram Pulse (Dal Chana) to a temple.
   - *The Physics:* Gram Pulse is **Jupiter**. Jupiter is the only planet that can save the Moon from the 8th House. By donating Jupiter, you call for the "Guru" to enter the "Grave" and rescue the disciple.

House 9: The Great Lake

(The Moon in Sagittarius: The Ocean of Dharma)

The Architecture of the Temple The 9th House is **Dhanu** (Sagittarius). It belongs to **Jupiter** (The Guru). It is the House of **Destiny** (*Bhagya*), **Ancestors** (*Pitra*), and **Pilgrimage**. When the Moon rises from the Grave (8th) and enters the 9th, it is a resurrection. It becomes **"The Great Lake." Jupiter (Air/Wisdom) + Moon (Water/Peace) = The Ocean.** This is considered one of the most auspicious placements in the *Lal Kitab*. The Moon here is not just water; it is *Holy Water* (*Charanamrit*).

The Dialogue: The Pilgrim's Luck

Aruna: "The view here is serene, O Light. The dark waters of the 8th are gone. I see a vast, blue ocean reflecting the sky. The air is filled with the sound of bells. Surely this native is blessed?"

Surya: "He is *Protected*, Aruna. The 9th House is the 'Pukka Ghar' (Permanent Home) of Jupiter. When the Moon enters Jupiter's house, she becomes the 'Queen in the Temple.' This native carries a spiritual safety net. When he falls, a cushion appears. When he is hungry, food arrives. Why? Because the 9th House is the house of **Ancestors**. A Moon in the 9th implies that the native's mother served the ancestors well. The 'Water' (Mother) has washed the 'Feet' (9th House) of the Elders."

The Parable of the Snake and the Milk

- **The Passenger:** A man who may not be outwardly religious, but is deeply moral. He is a traveler, a philosopher, or a judge.
- **The Destiny:** He has strange luck with travel. Whenever he goes on a pilgrimage, his wealth increases. He finds money in old coats. He is often the one who restores the family's honor.
- **The Flaw: The Neglected Altar.** The 9th House demands reverence. If the native lets his home altar become dirty, or if he keeps "broken images" of gods, the Ocean turns violent. **The Ancestral Warning:** Sometimes, the ancestors appear in the native's dreams as **Snakes**. This is not a bad omen here; it is a sign that the "Guardians of the Treasure" are thirsty.

The Remedial Logic: Feeding the Snakes

The remedy for the 9th House Moon is specific and mystical. It involves appeasing the forces that guard the Ancestral Ocean.

1. **Feeding Snakes with Milk:**
   - *The Prescription:* On **Nag Panchami** or specific lunar days, offer milk to snakes (or pour milk on a Shiva Lingam/Snake idol).
   - *The Alchemical Physics:* Snakes represent **Rahu** and **Ketu** (The Nodes). In the *Lal Kitab*, the Nodes are the "Guardians" of the 9th House threshold. The Moon (Milk) is the offering. Usually, Moon + Snake is an eclipse. But in the 9th House, the Snake is not biting; it is resting on Lord Vishnu's ocean (Sheshnag). It is docile. By feeding the Snake with Milk, you are harmonizing the **Moon** (Milk) with **Rahu** (Snake) under the supervision of **Jupiter** (9th House). You are turning the "Poison" of the Nodes into the "Protection" of the Ancestors. You are paying the toll to cross the ocean.
2. **The Saffron Tilak:**
   - *The Prescription:* Apply a Saffron (Kesar) mark on the forehead daily.
   - *The Physics:* Saffron is **Jupiter**. The Forehead is the **Ascendant**. By applying Jupiter to the head, you ensure the Moon (Mind) is constantly guided by Wisdom. It anchors the Ocean.
3. **The Square Silver Piece:**
   - *The Prescription:* Keep a square piece of silver in the pocket.
   - *The Physics:* **Silver** (Moon) + **Square** (Mars). The 9th House requires the courage of Mars to follow Dharma. This simple talisman gives the "Water" a "Brick" to stand on, ensuring the luck is solid, not fluid.

Summary Of The Waning Tide

Aruna looked back at the landscape of the Third Quadrant. He saw the chaotic Marketplace, the dark Crematorium, and the serene Ocean.

Aruna: "The Waning Tide is a journey of transformation, Surya. In the **7th**, the Moon fought the Wife—and learned to share the house through the Balance of the Scale. In the **8th**, the Moon faced Death—and learned to survive by vaccinating itself with the Water of the Grave. In the **9th**, the Moon met God—and learned that even the Ocean must feed the Snakes to remain holy."

Surya: "You see the truth, Charioteer. Peace is not just about comfort. Peace is about **Negotiation**. Negotiating with the Partner. Negotiating with Death. Negotiating with the Ancestors. But the journey is not over. The Chariot must now climb to the frozen peaks of the **Final Quadrant**. We enter the **Frozen Tide**. In the **10th**, the Moon freezes into Ice in the House of Karma. In the **11th**, she faces the Enemy's Court of Profit. In the **12th**, she becomes the Rain on the Roof. Prepare yourself, Aruna. The air is about to get very cold. We will learn why drinking milk at night can poison a King. Turn the page to **Chapter 7**."

CHAPTER 7: THE FROZEN TIDE

(The Moon in Houses 10, 11, and 12: The Final Quadrant)

The Ascent To The Glaciers

The Chariot rattled violently as it left the serene, blue waters of the 9th House. Aruna had grown accustomed to the calm of the "Great Lake," where the Moon was protected by the wisdom of Jupiter and the blessings of the Ancestors. The air there had been warm, filled with the scent of temple flowers and sandalwood.

But now, the road turned sharply upward.

The lush vegetation of the 9th House withered into brown scrub. The air grew thin, biting, and dangerously cold. The golden light of the Sun seemed to dim, filtered through a haze of gray frost. The wheels of the Chariot no longer rolled on soft earth; they ground against black volcanic rock and ice.

Aruna pulled his cloak tighter, his breath forming white clouds in the freezing air.

Aruna: "O Surya, the temperature is dropping rapidly. My hands are numb on the reins. The water in our vessels is beginning to crystallize. We have left the protection of the Temple. What lies in these frozen peaks? Why does the Moon feel so brittle here?"

Surya: "We are entering the **Final Quadrant**, Aruna. This is the **Frozen Tide**. In the 9th, the Moon was liquid and expansive—an Ocean of Grace. But here, we enter the domain of **Saturn** (Shani). In the **10th**, the Moon enters the fortress of **Karma**. Here, Water meets Rock. Emotion meets Duty. The liquid freezes into Ice. In the **11th**, the Moon enters the **Enemy's Court** of Profit. It is a slaughterhouse for peace. In the **12th**, the Moon evaporates into the **Rain of Moksha**. This is the hardest leg of the journey, Charioteer. In the warmth of the lower houses, the Moon could flow around obstacles. Here, she must harden or perish. Tighten your grip. We are about to meet the **Surgeon**."

House 10: The Frozen Lake

(The Moon in Capricorn: The Liquid Medicine)

The Architecture of the Fortress The 10th House is **Karma Sthan** (House of Action). It is the Zenith of the chart—the highest point in the sky at noon. It belongs to **Saturn** (Capricorn). It is the house of the Father's status, the Government, the Career, the Bones, and the cold, hard reality of the world. Saturn is cold, dry, and hard. The Moon is wet, soft, and emotional. When the Moon enters this fortress, she is stripped of her sentimentality. She cannot be a "Mother" here; she must become an "Executive." The *Lal Kitab* calls this placement **"The Frozen Lake"** or **"The Jar of Medicine."** Why Medicine? Because medicine is often bitter, cold, and precise—just like a Moon in the 10th House must be to survive.

The Dialogue: The Tears of the King

Aruna: "I see a King sitting on a throne of black basalt. He is powerful, commanding armies of workers. But his eyes are dry. He looks like a statue. Is the Moon dead here? Has the heart stopped beating?"

Surya: "She is not dead, Aruna; she is **Disciplined**. To rule the world (10th House), one cannot weep at every tragedy. The Moon in the 10th House converts 'Empathy' into 'Duty.' This native makes an excellent **Doctor**, **Surgeon**, or **Judge**. Think of a Surgeon. If he cried every time he saw blood (Moon), the patient would die. He must freeze his heart to steady his hand. He cares for the patient by cutting him open. This native shows love through *Provision*, not affection. He pays the bills, he protects the borders, he enforces the law. However, there is a terrible danger in this freezing process."

Aruna: "What danger?"

Surya: "The danger of the **Hollow Home.** The 10th House (Noon/Career) looks directly at the **4th House** (Midnight/Home). When the Moon sits in the 10th, the 4th House is often empty or neglected. This creates the **'King of the Office, Beggar of the Home'** syndrome. The native builds a massive empire, but his own mother falls sick, or he is separated from his family. The 'Water' has moved to the 'Workplace,' leaving the 'Home' dry. He is surrounded by employees but sleeps alone."

The Parable of the Poisoned Milk

- **The Passenger:** A high-ranking government official, a corporate CEO, or a strict patriarch. He works 18 hours a day. He is respected but feared. He rarely smiles. His life is a series of duties executed with military precision.
- **The Comfort:** He has one weakness. He loves milk. He drinks a glass of warm milk every night before bed to soothe his stress. He believes it is healthy.
- **The Collapse:** Slowly, his health deteriorates. He develops chronic chest congestion, asthma, or a deep, inexplicable depression. His eyesight fails (Moon rules the left eye). His career, once unshakeable, begins to stall. He feels like he is drowning in invisible sludge.
- **The Alchemical Physics:** This is one of the most critical laws of the *Lal Kitab*.
    - **Night** is the time of **Saturn**.
    - **Milk** is the **Moon**.
    - The 10th House is **Saturn's Fortress**.
    - When the native drinks Milk (Moon) at Night (Saturn), he is chemically mixing two enemies in his own body.
    - Saturn "curdles" the Moon. The result is **Liquid Poison** (*Zahar*).
    - For a Moon in 10 native, drinking milk at night is not nutrition; it is a slow suicide of the mind. It turns the "Ice" of his discipline into the "Slush" of depression.

The Remedial Logic: The Prohibition of the White Fluid

To survive the Frozen Lake, the native must respect the rigid laws of Saturn.

1. **The Milk Ban:**
   - *The Law:* **Never drink milk after sunset.**
   - *The Exception:* You can drink milk during the day (when the Sun warms the Moon). Or, you can drink Curd/Buttermilk (Venus forms) or Tea/Coffee (dry forms). But pure white milk at night is forbidden. It is like pouring water on a freezing engine; it will crack the block.
2. **The Pump Remedy:**
   - *The Law:* Do not keep a hand-pump, a borewell, or an exposed water source directly under the roof of the main house.
   - *The Physics:* The 10th House represents the **Foundation/Structure**. Pulling water from the dark earth (Saturn) *inside* the structure destabilizes the foundation. The water source should be outside the main walls. If the Moon is "under the roof" in the 10th, the roof collapses.
3. **The Alcohol Distributor:**
   - *The Prescription:* Paradoxically, the *Lal Kitab* says this native can become wealthy by *trading* in liquids like alcohol, petroleum, or chemicals.
   - *The Logic:*
     - Alcohol is **Saturn's Water** (Fermented/Old).
     - Medicine is **Saturn's Healing**.
     - Since the Moon is in Saturn's house, trading in "Saturnian Fluids" pleases the landlord.
   - *The Warning:* He must **never drink the alcohol himself**. If he drinks, the Saturn poison enters his Moon mind, and the ice will crack and drown him. He must be the Dealer, never the Addict.

House 11: The Enemy's Court

(The Moon in Aquarius: The Grandmother in the Shop)

The Architecture of the Profit Zone The 11th House is **Labh Sthan** (House of Gains). It belongs to **Saturn** (Aquarius) and **Jupiter** (Natural Ruler). It is the house of Social Networks, Elder Siblings, Ambition, and the fulfillment of desires. Superficially, it looks like a good place. It is the house of "Incoming." But in the *Lal Kitab*, the 11th House has a darker reputation for the Moon. The 11th House is the **8th from the 4th**. (Count: 4, 5, 6, 7, 8, 9, 10, 11 = 8 steps). The 8th House represents **Death**. Therefore, the 11th House represents the **Death of the 4th House**—the Death of the Mother, or the Death of Peace. When the Moon enters here, she is entering the **Enemy's Court**.

The Dialogue: The Hungry Ghost

Aruna: "This is the House of Profit, O Light. I see gold coins raining from the sky. Surely the Moon here brings wealth? Why do you call it the Enemy's Court?"

Surya: "It brings wealth, Aruna, but at a terrible price. Imagine a Grandmother (Moon) who should be resting at home, telling stories to her grandchildren. Instead, she is forced to sit in a noisy, crowded shop (11th House), haggling over pennies, fighting with customers, and counting profits. She is out of place. She is humiliated. Her softness is exploited by the market. The Moon in the 11th House is **The Hungry Ghost**. The native makes money, but he never feels 'full.' The peace of mind evaporates in the heat of ambition. He always wants 10% more. And worse —this placement endangers the **Mother**. Since the 11th is the 'Grave of the 4th,' the native often sees his mother suffer, or he has a difficult, transactional relationship with her. The more he chases profit, the sicker she becomes."

The Parable of the Trader of Toys

- **The Passenger:** A successful businessman, a socialite, or a network marketer. He has hundreds of friends (11th House rules circles). He is always at parties. He is charming but superficial.
- **The Conflict:** He wants a son (5th House). But the 11th House looks directly at the **5th House** (180-degree aspect).
  - Moon (Cold) in 11 casts a freezing gaze on the 5th (The Cradle/Sun's House).
  - *Result:* He struggles to conceive, or his children are weak, or they turn against him. The "Grandmother" (Moon) is fighting the "Grandchildren" (5th).
- **The Grandmother:** He forces his mother to live with him, but he treats her like a servant or a "Lucky Charm" for his business. He measures her value in gold.
- **The Crash:** He buys a house on a **Friday**.
  - *The Alchemical Physics:* Friday is **Venus**. Venus is the Enemy of the Moon. Building a house (Saturn) on a Venus day triggers a planetary war in the 11th House. His son falls ill immediately after the housewarming.

The Remedial Logic: The Sweet Offering to the Dark Lord

To protect the Mother and the Children, we must appease the Lord of the 11th House: **Bhairon** (The fierce form of Saturn). We must pay the tax of the Market.

1. **The Bhairon Temple Ritual:**
   - *The Prescription:* Offer **Kheer** (Sweet Rice Milk) to the Bhairon Temple on Saturdays.
   - *The Alchemical Physics:*
     - **Bhairon** is the deity of Saturn.
     - **Kheer** is Moon (Milk/Rice) + Mars (Sugar/Heat).
     - By offering the Moon to the Lord of the House, you pay the "Tax."
     - You are saying: "I acknowledge that this Profit belongs to you, Saturn. I am just the custodian. Take the sweetness, and spare my children."

    - This stops Saturn from attacking the 5th House (Children).

2. **The 121-Piece Remedy:**
    - *The Prescription:* Make **121** small pedas (sweet balls) of khoya/milk and donate them to young children or float them in the river.
    - *The Logic:* Why 121? Because 11 squared is 121. This is a mathematical remedy to "square" the debt of the 11th House. By giving the sweets to children (5th House), you strengthen the 5th House against the gaze of the 11th.
3. **Gold on the Body:**
    - *The Prescription:* Wear **Gold** (Jupiter) on the ears or neck.
    - *The Physics:* Jupiter is the only planet that can mediate between Moon and Saturn. Gold stabilizes the "Cloud" of the 11th House so it can rain profit without causing a storm.

House 12: The Rainwater

(The Moon in Pisces: The Roof of the World)

The Architecture of the Void The 12th House is **Vyaya Sthan** (House of Loss/Expense). It belongs to **Jupiter** (Pisces) and **Rahu** (The Void). It represents Sleep, Dreams, Foreign Lands, Hospitals, and the **Roof of the House**. When the Moon reaches here, the cycle ends. The River meets the Sea. The Water evaporates into the Sky. The *Lal Kitab* calls this placement **"The Rainwater on the Roof."** It is water that falls from the heavens—unpredictable, uncontrollable, and necessary.

The Dialogue: The Leaking Mind

Aruna: "We have reached the end, Surya. The 12th House is the house of Moksha. Does the Moon find peace here?"

Surya: "She finds *Solitude*, Aruna. In the 12th, the Moon is isolated. This native is a **Dreamer**. He lives in his head. The boundary between 'Real' and 'Imagined' is thin. If the Moon is good, he is a visionary, a meditator, a man who sleeps the sleep of the just. But if the Moon is afflicted (by Rahu or Saturn), the Roof leaks. The 'Rainwater' (External Emotions) seeps into the house (Mind). The native suffers from insomnia, nightmares, and a strange financial curse: **The more he saves, the more he loses.**"

Aruna: "How can saving cause loss? That defies logic."

Surya: "It follows the logic of the **Drain**. The 12th House is the House of Flow. It is designed to let things go. If you plug a drain, the water backs up and rots the pipes. If this native tries to hoard money under his mattress, the 12th House will create an 'Emergency'—a sickness, a theft, a breakdown—to force the money out. The only way to keep wealth here is to **Spend** it voluntarily."

The Parable of the Hoarder's Hole

- **The Passenger:** A man who is obsessed with saving money. He counts every penny. He refuses to spend on himself. He sleeps on a broken bed to save money on a new one.
- **The Curse:** Every time his savings reach a certain amount (e.g., 100,000), a disaster strikes. His car engine explodes. His roof collapses. A family member needs urgent surgery. The cost is exactly what he saved.
- **The Solution:** He must learn to **Circulate**.
    - *The Law:* "Expense is the anchor of Wealth." The 12th House Moon native must voluntarily spend money on good causes (Charity/Education/Travel). By creating a "Voluntary Drain," he stops the "Accidental Drain." If he gives 10% to charity, the Universe protects the remaining 90%.

The Remedial Logic: The Aniseed Filter

To fix the leaking roof and protect the sleep, we must strengthen the connection between Jupiter and Mars.

1. **The Saunf (Aniseed) Remedy:**
    - *The Prescription:* Keep **Saunf** (Aniseed) and **Sugar** under the pillow at night.
    - *The Alchemical Physics:*
        - Saunf is **Mars**. Sugar is **Mars**.
        - Mars is the friend of the Moon.
        - By keeping Mars under the head (Pillow/12th House), you give the Moon a "Bodyguard."
        - The nightmares (Rahu) and the anxiety (Mercury) cannot attack the sleeping mind if Mars is standing watch. It acts as a filter for the dreams.
2. **Rainwater Collection:**
    - *The Prescription:* Keep a glass jar of collected **Rainwater** in the house.
    - *The Physics:*
        - Rain is the purest form of the 12th House Moon.
        - By keeping it in the house, you are symbolically "catching the luck" that falls from the sky, rather than letting it drain away. You are domesticating the Rain.
3. **The Free Education Trap:**
    - *The Warning:* The native should **never** offer free education to others or pay for someone else's schooling out of charity.
    - *The Logic:* The 12th House is Jupiter (Education) + Moon (Money). Giving it away for free opens the sluice gate. It drains the native's own wisdom and wealth. He must charge a fee, even if it is symbolic, to close the energy circuit.

Summary Of The Frozen Tide

Aruna lowered the reins. The Chariot hovered at the peak of the Zodiac. They had traversed all twelve houses of the Moon. They had seen the Moon as a King, a Guest, a Warrior, a River, a Prophet, a Healer, a Merchant, a Ghost, an Ocean, a Surgeon, a Trader, and a Dreamer.

Aruna: "The journey of the Mind is exhausting, O Light. In the **10th**, the Moon froze into Duty, surviving only by rejecting the poison of the night. In the **11th**, she was sold in the Market, surviving only by paying the tax to the Dark Lord. In the **12th**, she dissolved into Rain, surviving only by learning to let go. Is there anything left?"

Surya: "The Mind is the vessel, Aruna. But the vessel is empty without the Wine. We have built the Chariot (Sun). We have cooled the Engine (Moon). Now, we must ask: **What is the destination?** Men do not live just to survive. They live to Enjoy. They live to Create. They live to Love. The Chariot must now turn toward the **Garden of Venus**. We must learn the physics of Desire. We must learn why Beauty is the most dangerous force in the universe. Prepare yourself. The scent of jasmine is approaching. We enter **Part III: The Garden of Venus**."

PART III: THE GARDEN OF VENUS

(The Path of Desire in the 12 Houses)

CHAPTER 8: THE SEED IN THE SOIL

(Venus in Houses 1, 2, and 3: The First Quadrant)

The Scent Of The Garden

The Chariot rattled violently as it left the frozen, crystalline peaks of the 12th House. For the last chapter of our journey, we had existed in the thin air of Moksha, where the Moon dissolved into the "Rain on the Roof." It was a place of solitude, loss, and sleep. It was cold.

But now, the horses flared their nostrils. The wheels struck soft, yielding earth.

The descent was rapid. The Chariot plunged from the ether into the atmosphere. The scent of ozone and ice vanished, replaced instantly by a heavy, intoxicating perfume. It smelled of wet black soil, blooming night-jasmine, crushed grapes, and the musk of animals. The air was thick, warm, and humid.

Aruna loosened his grip on the reins, wiping the sweat from his forehead.

Aruna: "O Surya, the world has transformed. The stark white snow is gone. Below us, I see lush, tangled gardens. I see marble palaces with open courtyards where fountains play day and night. I see lovers walking hand in hand in the shadows. The world feels... softer. And yet, my heart beats faster here than it did on the cliff edge. What is this place?"

Surya: "We have left the domain of the **Moon** (Chandra), Aruna. The Moon was *Need*—the water required to survive. A man drinks water because he must; if he does not, he dies. The Moon is the instinct of preservation. We now enter the domain of **Venus** (Shukra). Venus is *Want*—the wine required to enjoy. A man drinks wine not to survive, but to forget, or to remember, or to feel like a God. You have learned how to drive the Chariot (Sun). You have learned how to cool the engine (Moon). But now you must learn *why* the Chariot moves at all. Men do not conquer empires for water, Aruna. They possess water to survive, but they conquer empires for Gold, for Beauty, for Art, and for the promise of a Love that transcends death. **Venus is the Fuel of Desire.** Without Venus, the Chariot has a driver and an engine, but it has no destination. It has no 'Why.' Even the ascetic meditating in the cave desires God. That Desire is Venus."

Aruna: "But the scriptures say Desire is the root of suffering. Is this Garden a trap?"

Surya: "It is a trap, and it is a paradise. That is the paradox of Shukra. The Moon was a River; if you fell in, you could swim to the shore. Venus is a Quicksand perfumed with roses. If you fall in, you may struggle, but part of you will never want to leave. To master Venus is the hardest task of the Charioteer. To reject her is to be a stone. To indulge her is to be a beast. To *ride* her energy... that is to be a King. We begin our survey of the Garden now. In the **1st House**, Venus is the **Flower in the Fire**. In the **2nd**, she is the **Clay of Creation**. In the **3rd**, she is the **Siren in the Jungle**. Let us see how the Goddess of Love survives when she enters the House of the War God."

House 1: The Burning Flower

(Venus in the Ascendant: The Star of the Day)

The Architecture of the Paradox The 1st House is the **Lagna** (The Ascendant). It is the Throne. It is the exact moment of Sunrise. By the immutable cosmic law of the *Lal Kitab*, this house belongs to **Mars** (Aries) and is the exalted seat of the **Sun** (The King). It is a house of Fire, Red Blood, Iron, Bone, and Ego. It is the "I Am."

When **Venus**—the planet of softness, beauty, sperm, and luxury

—enters this house, it creates a magnificent astrological contradiction. Imagine a delicate orchid blooming in the middle of a burning battlefield. Or a beautiful Queen sitting on the Commander's saddle, wearing armor made of silk.

The *Lal Kitab* gives this placement a poetic and dangerous title: **"The Star of the Day"** (*Din ka Tara*). Venus is the Morning Star or the Evening Star. She is designed to shine in the twilight, when the Sun is weak. But in the 1st House (Sunrise), she dares to shine at noon. She defies the Sun.

The Dialogue: The Beautiful Tyrant

Aruna: "This seems fragile, Surya. Will the heat of the 1st House not burn the flower? Can Beauty survive the aggression of Mars and the blazing heat of the Sun?"

Surya: "She does not just survive, Aruna; she *conquers*. When Venus sits in the 1st House, the native is born with a magnetic shield. Mars (War) puts down his sword to look at her. This native does not need to fight to get their way. Their presence alone disarms the enemy. They are physically beautiful, charming, and immaculately dressed. They have a hypnosis in their eyes. When they walk into a room, the 'Heat' of the room drops. Everyone turns to look. However, there is a hidden cost."

Aruna: "What cost?"

Surya: "The cost of the **Boiling Fluid**. The 1st House is the **Body** (*Deh*). Venus is the **Semen/Biological Desire** (*Virya*). When the Fire of the 1st House (Mars/Sun) heats the Venus, the biological drive becomes hyper-active. The native becomes obsessed with their own image (Narcissism). They are obsessed with love, with validation, and with the pleasure of the senses. The 'Fire' boils the 'Fluid.' If this energy is not controlled, the Orchid burns. The native burns out young, exhausted by their own passions."

The Parable of the Prince Who Burned His Throne

- **The Passenger:** A handsome young man, the son of

a wealthy industrialist. He is charming, artistic, and the center of attention at every party. He dresses better than the King. He is the "Star of the Day."

- **The Conflict:** He falls in love at the age of 21. His passions (Venus in 1) are uncontrollable. He feels that without his lover, he will die. He defies his parents and marries in secret.
- **The Alchemy of Disaster:**
  - Marriage is the domain of **House 7**.
  - The 1st House looks directly at the 7th House (180-degree aspect).
  - By marrying at 21, he "Activates" the 7th House while his 1st House (Sun) is still immature.
  - He creates a direct energy circuit between the Fire (1st) and the Relationship (7th).
- **The Crash:** Within two years, the tragedy unfolds. His wife develops a mysterious illness. His own health collapses—he develops blood disorders or diabetes (Venus ailments). But the worst blow is to his **Career** (Sun). He loses interest in his work because he is consumed by the drama of his relationship. The Sun (Career) has been eclipsed by Venus (Desire).
- **The Law:** The *Lal Kitab* law is absolute here: **"If the Venus-in-1 native marries before the age of 25, the flower burns."**

The Remedial Logic: Cooling the Bed

To protect the flower from the fire, we must introduce the elements of Earth and Animal Service. We need to "ground" the static electricity of the 1st House.

1. **The Black Cow (Kapila Gaay):**
   - *The Prescription:* The native must serve a Black Cow (feed it or groom it), especially when going through marital strife.
   - *The Alchemical Physics:*
     - The Cow is the animal avatar of **Venus** (The Earthly Mother/Nourisher).

        - The color Black represents **Saturn**.
        - Saturn is the "Cooler" of Mars. Saturn is also the friend of Venus.
        - By serving a *Black* Cow, you are chemically binding the cooling discipline of Saturn to the passion of Venus. You are turning "Wild Lust" into "Service." It creates a protective, cooling layer around the flower.

2. **The Age of Maturation:**
    - *The Prescription:* Strictly **Do Not Marry before 25**.
    - *The Alchemical Physics:*
        - The Sun matures at age 22. The Moon matures at age 24.
        - The 1st House belongs to the Sun. You must wait for the "King" (Sun) to mature and take control of the Throne before you invite the "Queen" (Venus) to sit on it.
        - If you marry before 25, the Queen arrives while the King is still a boy. She dominates him, and the Kingdom (Life) falls into chaos.
3. **The Bathing Ritual:**
    - *The Prescription:* Add a spoonful of Curd (Yogurt) to the bathwater on Fridays.
    - *The Alchemical Physics:*
        - Curd is **Venus** in its fermented, earthy form.
        - The Body is the **1st House**.
        - This is a "Sympathetic Resonance" remedy. You are physically coating the 1st House (Body) with Venus (Curd) to harmonize the energy. Instead of the internal fire consuming the body, the body absorbs the cooling essence of Venus.

House 2: The Clay Of Creation

(Venus in Taurus: The Sher-Mukhi Wealth)

The Architecture of the Clay Pot The 2nd House is the **Dhan Sthan** (House of Wealth). It naturally belongs to **Venus** (Taurus), but its planetary landlord is **Jupiter** (The Guru). This is a home-coming. Venus is returning to her own zodiac sign (Taurus), which represents **Earth**, **Fixed Assets**, **Jewelry**, and the **Throat**. The *Lal Kitab* calls this the **"Goddess in the Temple."** It is one of the most powerful placements for material wealth in the entire Red Book. The text specifically refers to this house as **"Sher-Mukhi"** (Lion-Faced) when Venus is here.

The Dialogue: The Weaver of Gold

Aruna: "This must be a blessing, O Light. The Planet of Luxury in the House of Wealth. Surely this native sleeps on gold?"

Surya: "He sleeps on gold, Aruna, but his hands are covered in clay. The 2nd House is **Earth**. Venus is the **Art of Form**. When Venus sits here, the native has the Midas Touch, but specifically through *Tangible Creation*. He does not make money through abstract theory (Jupiter) or war (Mars). He makes money through **Pottery, Textiles, Farming, Jewels, or Architecture**. He takes the raw earth and makes it beautiful. He is the Weaver who turns thread into silk. He is the Jeweler who turns stone into a ring. However, there is a strange condition. The 2nd House is the **Face of the Mother** (Moon/Jupiter connection). It is the Temple of the Family. If the native creates wealth but disrespects the 'Producers' (Women/Labor), or if he brings Lust into the Temple, the clay crumbles back into dirt."

The Parable of the Potter's Palace

- **The Passenger:** A man born into poverty. He has no formal education. He starts working with clay, making simple pots or bricks.
- **The Destiny:** Slowly, his business grows. Unlike the Moon's wealth (which fluctuates like the tide), Venus's wealth in

the 2nd House is **Fixed**. It is heavy. He buys land. He buys gold. He builds a house that looks like a palace.

- **The Flaw: The Adulterous Tongue.**
    - The 2nd House is the **Voice** (*Vaani*).
    - If Venus in 2 is afflicted (e.g., by Rahu or Mars), the native uses "Sweet Words" to cheat people, especially women. He becomes a seducer. He creates "Fake Beauty."
- **The Karmic Backlash:** The *Lal Kitab* issues a terrifying warning: **"If the Venus-in-2 native commits adultery, his gold turns to dust."**
    - *The Logic:* The 2nd House is the 'Temple of the Family.' Venus here is the Goddess. You cannot bring Lust (Corrupt Venus) into the Temple. If he cheats on his wife, he desecrates the temple, and the Goddess leaves. The Lion (Sher-Mukhi) eats him.

The Remedial Logic: Potatoes, Turmeric, and the Blue Flower

To stabilize Venus in the 2nd House and harmonize her with the Landlord (Jupiter), we use the fruits of the Earth.

1. **The Potato and Turmeric Offering:**
    - *The Prescription:* Donate **Potatoes, Ghee**, and **Turmeric** (Haldi) to a temple.
    - *The Alchemical Physics:*
        - **Potato** is a tuber that grows underground. It is "Hidden Earth." It represents **Venus** (Sustenance).
        - **Turmeric** is Yellow. It represents **Jupiter** (The Landlord of the 2nd House).
        - **Ghee** is the lubricant (Venus).
        - By offering the Potato (Venus) coated in Turmeric (Jupiter) to the Temple (2nd House), you are chemically binding the "Luxury" to the "Dharma."
        - You are telling the Universe: "My wealth (Venus) serves the Guru (Jupiter)." This prevents

the wealth from becoming corrupt. It legalizes the gold.

2. **The Blue Flower in the Dirt:**
   - *The Prescription:* Take a Blue Flower (or a blue stone) and bury it in the mud/dirt.
   - *The Alchemical Physics:*
     - Blue is the color of **Rahu** (Obsession/Smoke).
     - Earth/Mud is **Venus/2nd House.**
     - Why bury Rahu? Because Rahu is the "Smoke" that clouds judgment and leads to adultery. By physically burying the Blue Flower in the Earth, you are "grounding" the Obsession. You are trapping the Demon (Rahu) in the Earth so that the pure Goddess (Venus) can shine without smoke.
3. **The Sher-Mukhi Architecture:**
   - *The Rule:* If this native builds a house, the front of the house should be **wider** than the back. This is called **Sher-Mukhi** (Lion-Faced).
   - *The Logic:* A Lion-Faced house accumulates energy. It resembles a seated lion, representing authority and accumulation. It resonates with the grandeur of Venus in the 2nd. A "Gau-Mukhi" (Cow-Faced/Narrow Front) house will choke his wealth.

House 3: The Deceptive Lover

(Venus in Gemini: The Siren in the Jungle)

The Architecture of the Trap The 3rd House is the **Jungle**. It belongs to **Mars** (Courage) and **Mercury** (Logic/Communication). When Venus enters here, she is no longer the Queen or the Goddess. She is stripped of her finery. She is **"The Dancing Girl in the Army Camp."** She is surrounded by soldiers (Mars) and spies (Mercury). She is safe only if she keeps dancing. If she stops, she is devoured. The *Lal Kitab* is deeply suspicious of this placement.

It calls it **"The Deceptive Beauty"** or **"The Sweet Poison."**

The Dialogue: The Seduction of Logic

Aruna: "I fear for her here, Surya. Beauty in the jungle is a target. Can she survive the aggression of the 3rd House?"

Surya: "She survives by becoming **The Manipulator**, Aruna. In the 3rd House, Venus loses her innocence. She learns to use her charm as a weapon. This native is incredibly persuasive. They can sell sand in the desert. They can convince a King to give up his crown. They are drawn to **Music, Writing, Acting, and Media**. They know how to play the strings of the human heart. But the mixture is volatile: **Mercury (Logic) + Mars (Aggression) + Venus (Lust) = The Scandal.** The native often gets involved in complicated love triangles. They use their siblings or neighbors to hide their affairs. They thrive on the thrill of the chase. But remember, Aruna: The Hunter often becomes the Hunted."

The Parable of the Musician's Scandal

- **The Passenger:** A gifted artist, writer, or influencer. They have a mesmerizing voice. They play musical instruments beautifully.
- **The Destiny:** They gain fame early. People fall in love with their words.
- **The Crisis:** The 3rd House looks directly at the **9th House** (Luck/Father/Dharma).
    - If the native falls into debauchery (Corrupt Venus)—seducing the spouses of friends or neighbors—the 9th House collapses.
    - *The Result:* The father suffers a heart attack. Or the native's luck vanishes overnight. We see this in celebrities who destroy their massive careers through one foolish sex scandal. The "Jungle" swallows them.
- **The Musical Trigger:** The *Lal Kitab* has a strange warning here: **"Musical Instruments in the house act as a trigger."**
    - *The Physics:* Music is the language of Venus. But instru-

ments function through **Vibration** (Mercury/Air).

- If the native is morally weak, keeping many instruments (especially stringed ones like Guitars/Sitars) vibrates the air with Venus energy.
- If Mars (3rd House) is malefic, this vibration turns into "War Drums" rather than "Love Songs." The arguments in the house increase. The vibration of the instrument disturbs the peace of the home.

The Remedial Logic: The Silver Chain and the Sister

To protect the native from their own charm, we must introduce the Moon (Mother/Decency) to cool the Mars-Venus heat.

1. **Respect Women (The Universal Shield):**
   - *The Prescription:* Strictly avoid flirting with maidservants, neighbors, or the spouses of friends. Treat them as "Mother" or "Sister."
   - *The Physics:* This is not just moral; it is mechanical. By re-classifying these women as "Sister" (Mercury) or "Mother" (Moon), you deactivate the Venus (Lover) frequency. You disarm the bomb.
2. **The Silver Ornament:**
   - *The Prescription:* The native's spouse should wear a **Silver Bracelet** or **Chain.**
   - *The Alchemical Physics:*
     - Silver is **Moon.**
     - The Moon controls Venus (Mother controls the Daughter-in-law).
     - Wearing silver cools the "Jungle Heat." It acts as a leash on the wandering mind. It reminds the native of the "Home" (Moon) whenever they are tempted by the "Jungle" (Venus).
3. **Serve the Uncle:**
   - *The Prescription:* Serve the maternal uncle (Mama).
   - *The Physics:* The 3rd House is the house of the Uncle (Mercury). Keeping good relations here stabilizes the

Mercury factor, preventing the "Spy" from betraying the "Dancing Girl."

Summary Of The First Quadrant Of Desire

Aruna looked down at the Garden. He saw the scorched flower in the 1st, the golden pot in the 2nd, and the dancing girl in the 3rd.

Aruna: "The Garden is treacherous, Surya. In the **1st**, Desire burns the Self. In the **2nd**, Desire builds the Wealth—but only if the hands are clean. In the **3rd**, Desire seduces the Mind—but only if the song remains pure."

Surya: "Desire is a vine, Aruna. It grows where you plant it. If you plant it in Fire (1st), it burns. If you plant it in Earth (2nd), it fruits. If you plant it in the Jungle (3rd), it strangles. But the vine keeps growing. It is the life force itself. Now, the Chariot moves to the **Second Quadrant**. Venus must now enter the **Domestic Sphere**. She must face the **Mother in the 4th**. She must face the **Child in the 5th**. And she must face the **Enemy in the 6th**. Prepare yourself. We are about to see what happens when the Lover enters the Kitchen. Turn the page to **Chapter 9**."

CHAPTER 9: THE DOMESTIC GARDEN

(Venus in Houses 4, 5, and 6: The Second Quadrant)

The Entrance To The Inner Court

The Chariot rattled and slowed as it left the wild, tangled jungle of the 3rd House. For the last leg of the journey, the horses had been skittish, reacting to the invisible tigers and the constant, low-level hum of anxiety that permeated the domain of the "Green Moon." The air there had been thick with the scent of musk, intrigue, and the sharp, metallic tang of adrenaline. It was a place where peace had to be fought for with a sword, and love was often a trap laid by a hunter.

But now, as the celestial wheels turned forward, crossing the invisible boundary into the Second Quadrant, the landscape underwent a profound transformation.

The dense canopy of creeper vines receded. The ground leveled out into smooth, paved courtyards. The chaotic noise of the marketplace faded into a respectful silence, broken only by the sound of water splashing in fountains and the distant, rhythmic chanting of prayers.

Ahead of the Chariot lay a view that stole the breath from the Charioteer's lungs. It was not the wild beauty of nature, but the cultivated beauty of civilization. He saw walled gardens where roses bloomed in neat rows. He saw white marble houses with open verandas. He smelled the comforting aroma of baking bread, fresh linen drying in the sun, and the sweet smoke of hearth fires.

Aruna loosened the reins, his shoulders dropping inches as the tension left his body.

Aruna: "O Surya, the landscape has changed again. We have left the outer world—the burning throne of the 1st, the bank of the 2nd, and the dangerous jungle of the 3rd. We are now entering a walled garden. I see homes with courtyards, schools with children playing in safety, and wells where women gather to talk.

This feels private. This feels... intimate."

Surya: "It is intimate, Aruna. We have entered the **Second Quadrant**—the **Domestic Sphere**. Here, Venus is no longer a public figure. She is not the Queen on the Throne, dazzling the court with her brilliance. She is not the Dancer in the Camp, seducing the soldiers with her movements. Here, Venus takes off her crown and her anklets. She becomes the **Wife**, the **Lover**, and the **Healer**. In the **4th House**, she enters the **Kitchen of the Mother**. In the **5th House**, she enters the **Playground of the Child**. In the **6th House**, she enters the **Well of the Servant**. This is the heart of the chart. This is where the private life of the native is written. But remember, Charioteer: **Fire in the Kitchen burns the house down.** Desire is dangerous in public, but it is fatal in private. If Venus is corrupted here, the home becomes a prison. The bedroom becomes a battlefield. Let us see what happens when the Goddess of Love tries to become a Housewife."

House 4: The Two Wives

(Venus in Cancer: The Drowning Lover)

The Architecture of the Conflict The 4th House is **Kark** (Cancer). By natural law, it belongs to the **Moon**. It is the **River**. It is the **Mother's Lap**. It is the seat of **Sukh** (Peace), **Ancestral Property**, and the **Heart**. It is the foundation upon which the entire horoscope rests. When **Venus** (The Wife/Lover/Luxury) enters here, she is entering the territory of the **Moon** (The Mother/Nurturer).

In the deep mythology of the *Lal Kitab*, the Moon and Venus are enemies. They represent two different, often competing types of feminine energy:

- **The Moon:** Nurturing, unconditional, protective, fluid, self-sacrificing. She is the Mother who feeds the child before herself.
- **Venus:** Desiring, conditional, pleasurable, material, demanding. She is the Wife who demands the husband's attention and resources.

When they are forced into the same room (the 4th House), a war begins. It is not a war of swords, but a silent, suffocating war fought over the heart of the native. The *Lal Kitab* calls this placement **"Two Swords in One Sheath"** or **"Two Wives for One Husband."**

The Dialogue: The War of the Women

Aruna: "I see two women standing in the courtyard, Surya. One holds a cup of milk (Moon), and the other holds a mirror of beauty (Venus). They are not speaking to each other. The air is thick with tension. Can they not coexist? Does the Chariot not need both Nurturance and Love to move forward?"

Surya: "They can coexist, Aruna, but it requires a saint to manage them. The Native with Venus in the 4th often faces a deep psychological crisis: **The Wife vs. The Mother.** His wife tries to take over the role of the Mother. She wants to rule the domestic sphere. She rearranges the kitchen. She demands his total attention. She wants to be the center of his emotional world. But the Mother (Moon) resists. She feels displaced in her own home. She feels her son is being stolen by a 'Stranger.' She uses guilt as a weapon. This conflict tears the native apart. He wants to love his wife, but his loyalty to his mother makes him feel guilty. He becomes a pendulum swinging between two poles of feminine power. And there is a darker danger here."

Aruna: "What danger?"

Surya: "The Poisoning of the Guru. Jupiter is exalted in the 4th House. Jupiter represents Wisdom, Ethics, and the 'Breath of Life.' Venus hates Jupiter. She is the Demon Guru (*Daitya Guru*), and he is the Divine Guru (*Deva Guru*). When Venus sits in the 4th, she poisons the Jupiter energy. The *Lal Kitab* says: **'The Native will be wealthy, but his character will be stained.'** He may seek peace in addiction—Drugs, Alcohol, or excessive Luxury—because he cannot find peace in the arms of either woman. He drowns his sorrow in the very liquid that should sustain him. The River becomes a flood of intoxication."

The Parable of the Second Marriage

- **The Passenger:** A man who is outwardly successful. He deals in real estate, vehicles, or agriculture (all 4th House domains). He lives in a beautiful house near a lake or river. He is charming, emotional, and deeply attached to his comforts. He drives a luxury car (Venus) but listens to sad songs (Moon).
- **The Flaw:** He is never satisfied with one partner. The "Water" of the 4th House dilutes the "Fire" of loyalty. The Moon (Fluctuation) makes his Venus (Love) unstable. He seeks the "Mother" in his "Wife," and when he doesn't find her, he looks elsewhere.
- **The Curse: "Two Marriages"** (*Do Shadi*).

  - The *Lal Kitab* warns that Venus in the 4th often indicates that the first marriage will end in divorce or death, or the native will keep a mistress.
  - *The Physics:* The 4th House represents the "Resting Place." If Venus (Desire) is restless there, the domestic peace is shattered. The native brings his "Lover" into the "Sanctuary," desecrating it. The bed is never cold, but the heart is never warm.
- **The Career Impact:** The 4th House casts a direct aspect on the **10th House** (Career/Sun).
  - If the native brings a mistress home, or indulges in excessive luxury (drugs/alcohol) at home, the "Smoke" from the 4th House rises to the 10th House.
  - The 10th House is the Sun. The Smoke blinds the Sun.
  - *Result:* The powerful businessman loses his reputation because of his private life. His "Night" destroys his "Day." A scandal erupts that washes away his empire.

The Remedial Logic: The Horse and the Well

To save the domestic peace, we must separate the Wife (Venus) from the Mother (Moon) and protect the Guru (Jupiter). We must legalize the desire and anchor the home with the authority of the Sun.

1. **The Remarriage Ritual:**
  - *The Prescription:* The native should "remarry" his own wife.
  - *The Alchemical Physics:*
    - This ritual involves the couple exchanging garlands again, or changing the wife's name legally.
    - This acts as a "System Reset." It tricks the planetary energy into thinking a "Second Marriage" has occurred, satisfying the prophecy of "Two Marriages" without the need for a divorce. It is a loophole in the Cosmic Law to save the family structure.

2. **Throwing Copper in the River:**
   - *The Prescription:* Throw a **Copper Coin** (or a square Copper piece) into a flowing river for 43 days continuously.
   - *The Alchemical Physics:*
     - **Copper** is the metal of the **Sun**.
     - **River** is the **Moon/4th House.**
     - Why Sun? Because the Sun is the King. When the King enters the room, the two fighting Queens (Moon and Venus) stop fighting and bow.
     - The Sun brings order to the 4th House chaos. It gives the "Water" a "spine." It introduces Authority into the Home, stopping the emotional manipulation.
3. **The Well Remedy:**
   - *The Prescription:* Drop a **Yellow Flower** or **Gram Lentils** (Chana Dal) into a well.
   - *The Alchemical Physics:*
     - **Yellow** represents **Jupiter.**
     - Venus in 4 tries to kill Jupiter (Exalted in 4).
     - By feeding Jupiter items (Yellow) to the "Water Source" (Well), you ensure the Guru stays alive amidst the flood of desire. You ensure that Wisdom survives Lust. You are feeding the "Spirit" so it doesn't drown in the "Flesh."

House 5: The Padmini (The Lotus Woman)

(Venus in Leo: The Burning Romance)

The Architecture of the Court The 5th House is **Simha** (Leo). It belongs to the **Sun**. It is the House of the King, the Divine Intellect, the Progeny, and **Romance** (*Prem*). When Venus enters here, she is the **"Padmini"**—the most beautiful woman in the court. She is the Queen of Hearts. This placement creates a magnetic, charismatic lover. The native falls in love with the intensity of the Sun. They love grand gestures, poetry, and drama. They want a love story that will be written in history books. However, the Sun (King) is a jealous lover. He demands total submission. The *Lal Kitab* warns: **"Love will destroy the Throne."**

The Dialogue: The King's Distraction

Aruna: "The garden here is bathed in sunlight, Surya. The flowers are bright red and gold. It looks like a place of joy. Why do you frown? Is love not a noble pursuit for a King?"

Surya: "Because Fire burns Flowers, Aruna. The 5th House is the house of **Future** and **Career Foundation**. It is the sun that ripens the crops. When Venus sits here, the native becomes obsessed with Romance. He is the King who forgets to rule because he is writing poetry for his lover. He ignores his advisors (Jupiter) to listen to his mistress (Venus). The 'Heat' of the 5th House amplifies the 'Desire' of Venus. The native chases love at the cost of his dignity. He becomes a slave to beauty. He makes decisions based on passion, not policy. And the Sun exacts a heavy price for this negligence. The *Lal Kitab* law is: **'If the Venus-in-5 native indulges in love affairs, his career (Sun) turns to ash.'** This is the placement of the **Scandalous Lover**. The higher the passion, the harder the fall."

The Parable of the Politician's Fall

- **The Passenger:** A rising politician, a student with a brilliant future, or a gifted artist. He has the "Sun" in his destiny —leadership potential. He is destined for greatness.
- **The Distraction:** He falls madly in love. He is not discreet. He flaunts his partner. He spends his time in leisure, neglecting his duties. He skips exams to meet his lover. He misses crucial meetings to buy flowers.
- **The Padmini Curse:** The term *Padmini* refers to a woman of exceptional beauty who brings destruction to kingdoms (like Helen of Troy or Rani Padmini).

- The native's lover becomes the source of his downfall. A scandal erupts. His secrets are exposed. The very thing he loved destroys his reputation. His enemies use his love against him.

- **The Ancestral Debt:** Venus in the 5th often indicates a **Pitra Dosha** related to women. An ancestor may have mistreated a woman, and now that karma returns to block the native's progeny or happiness. The "Family Sun" is eclipsed by the "Venusian Shadow."

The Remedial Logic: Serving the Cow and the Ancestors

To cool the burning romance and save the career, we must introduce the element of Service. We must turn "Passion" into "Compassion." We must transform the Lover into the Devotee.

1. **Serve the Cow (Gau Sewa):**
   - *The Prescription:* Feed cows regularly, especially white cows or the Kapila (Black) cow.
   - *The Alchemical Physics:*
     - The Cow is the Earthly, maternal form of **Venus**.
     - By serving the Cow, you transform the energy of Venus from "Lust/Romance" to "Dharma/Service."
     - You tell the Universe: "I honor Venus as a Mother, not just a Lover." This cools the 5th House fire. It pays the debt to the ancestors. It shifts the energy from the genitals to the heart.
2. **Clean the Ancestral Altar:**
   - *The Prescription:* Maintain strict cleanliness in the home temple. Keep the West side of the house (Saturn's direction) clean.
   - *The Alchemical Physics:*
     - The 5th House is the Sun (Ancestors).
     - Venus in 5 can pollute the ancestral line with scandal.
     - By cleaning the altar, you remove the "stain" of

Venus from the Sun's house. You restore the purity of the lineage.

3. **Marriage over Affair:**
   - *The Rule:* The native must marry his lover.
   - *The Logic:* If the relationship remains illicit (Rahu/Venus), it burns the Sun. If it is legalized into marriage (7th House energy), it stabilizes. A Venus in 5 native should never have casual flings; the karmic cost is too high. Marriage creates a container for the fire.

House 6: The Barefoot Beauty

(Venus in Virgo: The Wife Without Shoes)

The Architecture of the Valley The 6th House is **Kanya** (Virgo). It belongs to **Mercury** and **Ketu**. It is the House of Service, Sickness, Debt, Litigation, and the **Underworld**. Here, Venus is **Debilitated** (*Neecha*). She is the **"Barefoot Beauty."** Imagine a Queen forced to walk on thorns without shoes. She is stripped of her luxury. She is humbled. She wears rags instead of silk. This is a difficult placement. It indicates a wife who suffers, or a man who loses his wealth through women or health issues.

The Dialogue: The Humiliated Goddess

Aruna: "This is a sad place, O Light. The garden is overgrown with weeds. The ground is rocky and sharp. I see a beautiful woman walking barefoot, her feet bleeding. Why is she punished here? What crime has Beauty committed?"

Surya: "She is not punished; she is **Grounded**, Aruna. In the 6th House, Venus loses her vanity. She becomes the **Servant** or the **Nurse**. The native often marries a woman who is from a humble background, or who suffers from chronic health issues. Or, the native himself has a 'Servant's Mentality' towards love—he loves those who do not love him back. He gives, but receives nothing.

He washes the feet of those who kick him. The danger here is **Poverty**. Venus is **Liquid Cash** (Lakshmi). The 6th House is **Debt**. When Lakshmi falls into the pit of Debt, the money vanishes. The native earns, but the expenses (illness/enemies) eat it all. The bucket has a hole. But there is a secret key to unlock this prison."

Aruna: "What key?"

Surya: "The Golden Clip. The 6th House is ruled by Mercury and Ketu. To save Venus here, we need the help of **Jupiter** (Gold) and **Mars** (Courage)."

The Parable of the Bankrupt Husband

- **The Passenger:** A hard-working man who cannot save money. He works two jobs but is always in debt. His wife is constantly ill (reproductive issues or skin allergies—Venus domains).
- **The Symbolism:** His wife prefers to walk barefoot in the house. She hates wearing jewelry. She dresses plainly. She feels unworthy of luxury. She saves every penny but spends it on doctors.
- **The Diagnosis:** By walking barefoot, she is connecting directly with the "Earth of the 6th House" (Mercury/Ketu). She is grounding her Venus energy into the pit. She is acting out the role of the "Barefoot Beauty." She is absorbing the negative energy of the house through her soles.
- **The Crash:** The husband's business fails. He borrows money (6th House) to pay for her medical bills. The cycle of debt begins. The more he works, the deeper he sinks.

The Remedial Logic: The Golden Hair Clip

To save the wife and the wealth, we must elevate the status of Venus using **Jupiter** and **Mars**. We must crown the Queen and protect her feet.

1. **The Gold Hair Clip:**

- *The Prescription:* The wife **must** wear a **Gold Clip** (or Gold Pin) in her hair at all times.
- *The Alchemical Physics:*
  - **Gold** is **Jupiter**.
  - **Hair** is **Saturn/Rahu**.
  - The 6th House is the enemy of Venus.
  - By placing Gold (Jupiter) on the Head, you bring the "Guru" to protect the "Wife."
  - Jupiter neutralizes the poison of the 6th House. It gives Venus "Status." It tells the Universe: "This woman is not a servant; she is a Queen under the protection of the Guru." It elevates her energy from the feet to the crown.

2. **Shoes are Mandatory:**

- *The Rule:* The wife must **never** walk barefoot, even inside the house. She must wear slippers or shoes.
- *The Alchemical Physics:*
  - **Shoes** represent **Saturn** (Protection) or **Mars** (Leather).
  - By wearing shoes, she insulates herself from the "Earth of the 6th House." She stops the drain of energy. She literally "elevates" Venus above the dust. She breaks the circuit of grounding.

3. **Feed Young Girls:**

- *The Prescription:* Feed six young girls (Kanyas) sweets on Fridays.
- *The Alchemical Physics:*
  - The 6th House belongs to **Mercury** (Young Girls).
  - By feeding them, you appease the Landlord of the house. You turn the "Enemy" into a "Friend." You pay the rent so that Venus can live in peace.

Summary Of The Domestic Garden

Aruna looked back at the Domestic Quadrant. He saw the fighting queens in the 4th, the burning romance in the 5th, and the barefoot beauty in the 6th.

Aruna: "The Garden is a place of struggle, Surya. In the **4th**, Venus fought for territory. In the **5th**, Venus fought for attention. In the **6th**, Venus fought for dignity."

Surya: "It is the struggle of **Integration**, Aruna. Love cannot remain a fantasy. It must survive the Kitchen, the Nursery, and the Hospital. If it survives these three tests, it becomes real. But the journey is not over. The Chariot must now move to the **Third Quadrant**. Venus must enter the **Marketplace of the 7th**. She must descend into the **Grave of the 8th**. And she must climb the **Mountain of the 9th**. Prepare yourself. We are about to see what happens when the Goddess of Love meets the God of Death. Turn the page to **Chapter 10**."

CHAPTER 10: THE DANGEROUS BEAUTY

(Venus in Houses 7, 8, and 9: The Third Quadrant)

The Departure From The Walled Garden

The Chariot groaned and lurched as it left the manicured lawns of the 6th House. For the last leg of the journey, the horses had been walking on the soft, damp earth of the "Barefoot Beauty." They had witnessed the quiet struggle of Venus to maintain her dignity in the House of Service, where she acted as a nurse to the sick and a servant to the debt. It was a place of humility, where the Goddess wore no crown.

But now, the iron gates of the Domestic Garden swung open.

The road ahead changed instantly. The soft earth was replaced by hard, uneven cobblestones. The air grew thicker, heavier, filled with the roar of commerce, the smell of burnt offerings, the clinking of coins, and the distant, rhythmic sound of temple bells. The private world of the Family—the kitchen, the nursery, the well—was left behind.

Ahead lay the Public World. Ahead lay the Zone of Interaction.

Aruna tightened his grip on the reins. He felt a vibration in the wood of the Chariot—a low, humming frequency that made his teeth ache. It was the vibration of Ambition. It was the hum of a million souls bargaining for love and gold.

Aruna: "O Surya, the air here is electric. It feels charged with danger and opportunity. We have left the safe enclosure of the Home. The walls are gone. Where are we going? The horses are restless; they smell something metallic."

Surya: "We are entering the **Third Quadrant**, Aruna. This is the **Zone of Interaction**. Here, Venus is no longer just a Wife or a Lover. She becomes a Force of Nature. She becomes the Goddess who demands a price. In the **7th House**, she enters her own Palace—the **Marketplace of Marriage**. But power corrupts, and beauty can turn into pride. The Goddess becomes a Statue. In the

8th House, she descends into the **Volcano of Secrets**. Here, love becomes a burning chariot that can consume the soul. The Goddess becomes the Destroyer. In the **9th House**, she climbs the **Mountain of Dharma**. Here, the Lover must become the Pilgrim. The Goddess becomes the Devotee. This is the most dangerous leg of the journey. In the 7th, Venus can become a **Bronze Idol**—beautiful but cold. In the 8th, she can become a **Black Widow**—deadly and secretive. In the 9th, she can become a **Saint**—or a Hypocrite. Drive carefully, Charioteer. The road is slippery with oil and blood."

House 7: The Bronze Idol

(Venus in Libra: The Pride of Possession)

The Architecture of the Marketplace The 7th House is **Tula** (Libra). It is the natural home of **Venus**. It is the House of **Marriage, Partnership, Trade**, and **Open Enemies**. Here, Venus is in her own sign (*Swakshetra*). She is the Queen in her own castle. Superficially, this looks perfect. A Queen in her castle should be happy. She should be benevolent. She should be ruling with grace. But the *Lal Kitab* gives a chilling, paradoxical warning: **"The Bronze Idol."**

Why Bronze? Bronze is a hard alloy. It is shiny, beautiful, and durable, but it is cold. It does not yield. It does not breathe. The element of the 7th House is **Air** (Libra), but the element of Venus is **Earth/Water**. When Venus dominates here, the "Air" turns into a "Storm" of demands. The Earth turns into Metal. The native becomes obsessed with the *image* of the relationship, rather than the substance. The marriage becomes a display case.

The Dialogue: The Statue that Demands Blood

Aruna: "I see a beautiful woman sitting on a throne in the center of the marketplace. Men are throwing gold at her feet. She smiles, but her eyes are cold. She does not move. Is this not the Goddess of Love?"

Surya: "She is the Goddess of **Validation**, Aruna. In the 7th House, Venus often creates a native (male or female) who treats their partner as a **Trophy**. They want a spouse who looks good on their arm. They want a partner who increases their status in society. They want a mirror that reflects their own glory. But because Venus is 'Bronze' here, she lacks warmth. The native becomes proud. They think, 'I am the prize. You are lucky to have me. Worship me.' And this pride destroys the marriage. The *Lal Kitab* says: **'If the native is proud of his wife's beauty, he will lose his wealth.'** The 7th House is also the house of **Daily Income** (*Rozgar*). If the relationship turns cold (Bronze), the cash flow freezes. The partner becomes an idol that demands worship but gives nothing back. The gold coins thrown at her feet disappear into the void."

The Parable of the Merchant's Trophy

- **The Passenger:** A successful businessman. He is handsome, wealthy, and ambitious. He marries a stunningly beautiful woman (Venus in 7). She is the envy of his friends.
- **The Pride:** He shows her off at parties. He buys her expensive clothes, not because she needs them, but because they reflect *his* success. He interrupts her when she speaks. He treats her like a possession, a piece of living furniture.
- **The Decay:** Slowly, the "Bronze" nature takes over. The wife becomes distant. She develops health issues—usually related to the skin or reproductive system (Venus domains) —or she becomes domineering. She starts controlling his business decisions with a cold logic that ruins him. She spends his money to punish him.
- **The Bronze Effect:** The native finds that despite his wealth, he has no peace. His partners cheat him. His public image cracks. The "Bronze Idol" has fallen on him and crushed him.

- **The Contrast:** If he had treated her with humility—if he had seen her as a Soul (Sun) rather than a Body (Venus)—she would have been his greatest asset. She would have been Lakshmi. But he made her an Idol, and Idols do not speak; they only take offerings.

The Remedial Logic: The Blue Flower and the Living Cow

To melt the Bronze Idol and bring warmth back to the relationship, we must use the elements of **Earth** (Service) and **Water** (Moon). We must "ground" the Air of Libra and humble the Pride.

1. **The Blue Flower Ritual:**
   - *The Prescription:* Bury a **Blue Flower** in the mud/earth in a deserted place.
   - *The Alchemical Physics:*
     - **Blue** is the color of **Rahu** (Obsession/Smoke/Pride).
     - **Earth** is **Venus.**
     - Why bury Rahu? Because the "Pride" and "Obsession" in the 7th House are actually traits of Rahu (who co-rules the 7th in some texts as the agent of desire).
     - By physically burying the Blue Flower in the Earth, you are "grounding" the arrogance. You are trapping the demon of Pride in the soil.
     - You are telling the Universe: "I bury my ego. Let the pure Venus shine without the smoke of pride."
2. **Service to the Cow (Gau Sewa):**
   - *The Prescription:* Serve a **Red or Brown Cow.**
   - *The Alchemical Physics:*
     - The Cow is the **Living Venus.**
     - The Bronze Idol is the **Dead Venus.**
     - By serving the living animal (feeding/grooming), you breathe life back into the archetype. You shift from "Possession" to "Care."

- The Cow eats the "Grass" (Mercury/Trade) and gives "Milk" (Moon/Peace). This harmonizes the 7th House (Trade) with the 4th House (Peace). It teaches the native that love is service, not ownership.

3. **The Bronze Utensil Warning:**
   - *The Rule:* Do not keep large, decorative bronze statues or utensils in the bedroom. They amplify the cold, metallic energy of the 7th House. Use Copper (Sun) or Silver (Moon) instead.

House 8: The Burning Chariot

(Venus in Scorpio: The Secret Fire)

The Architecture of the Volcano The 8th House is **Vrishchik** (Scorpio). It belongs to **Mars** (Death/Passion) and **Saturn** (Longevity). It is the **Cremation Ground**. It is the house of **Secrecy**, **Occult**, **Scandal**, **Sudden Events**, and **Legacies**. When Venus enters here, she is **"The Burning Chariot."** Imagine a beautiful carriage engulfed in flames, racing toward a cliff at midnight. Venus (Lover) in the House of Mars (Passion) creates an intense, secretive, and often destructive sexual energy. The *Lal Kitab* calls this placement **"The Wife in the Grave"** or **"The Secret Lover."**

The Dialogue: The Kiss of the Scorpion

Aruna: "The air here is hot and sulphurous, Surya. I see lovers meeting in the dark, hiding their faces. I hear whispers of betrayal. Why is Love hiding in the grave? Why does Venus seek the darkness?"

Surya: "Because it is **Forbidden**, Aruna. Venus in the 8th House seeks intensity that the daylight cannot provide. The native is bored by 'normal' love. They are drawn to secret affairs, taboo relationships, or partners who are 'dangerous' or broken. They crave the adrenaline of the forbidden. But the 8th House is also the house of **Debt** and **Death**. When Venus burns here, she burns the native's assets. The *Lal Kitab* law is: **'The native will be destroyed by his own secrets.'** If he indulges in adultery, his wife will fall ill, or he will face a financial scandal that wipes out his legacy. And yet... if this energy is sublimated... Venus here can become the **Tantric Healer**. She can navigate the darkness to find the soul. She can transform poison into medicine."

The Parable of the Ruined Heir

- **The Passenger:** A man who inherits wealth (8th House rules inheritance/Wills). He is married, but he feels "dead" in his marriage. He craves excitement.
- **The Spark:** He meets a woman who is mysterious, perhaps troubled (8th House archetype). She carries the scent of danger. He starts a secret affair. He feels alive only in the dark.
- **The Fire:** The affair consumes him. He spends his inheritance on her. He lies to his family. He becomes paranoid (8th House shadow).
- **The Explosion:** The 8th House rules **Sudden Events**. The affair is exposed in a humiliating way. His wife attempts suicide (Venus affliction). His creditors come calling. The Chariot burns, and he is trapped inside.
- **The Warning:** The *Lal Kitab* warns that the native's wife should **never walk barefoot** on the damp earth. The 8th House is the "Damp Earth." If she connects with it, her energy drains into the grave.

The Remedial Logic: The Blue Flower and the Copper Coin

To extinguish the fire of the 8th House, we must use **Cooling Agents** and **Grounding Agents**. We must flush the poison before it kills the host.

1. **The Blue Flower in the Drain:**
   - *The Prescription:* Throw a **Blue Flower** (or a piece of

lead/Ranga) into a dirty drain or sewer (*Ganda Naala*) for 43 days continuously.

- *The Alchemical Physics:*
  - **Blue Flower** represents **Rahu/Venus** energy (The Obsession/Lust/Secret Desire).
  - **The Drain** is the physical manifestation of the **8th House** (Waste/Underworld).
  - By voluntarily throwing the "Flower of Desire" into the "Drain," you are ritually enacting the loss.
  - You are telling the 8th House: "I sacrifice this toxic desire. Do not take my real life. Do not take my wife."
  - This flushes the secretive energy out of the system before it can explode in the native's face.

2. **The Copper Coin in the Crematorium:**

- *The Prescription:* Throw a **Copper Coin** into a burning pyre (if possible) or bury it near a cremation ground.
- *The Alchemical Physics:*
  - **Copper** is the metal of the **Sun**.
  - The Sun is the King.
  - When the King enters the Crematorium (8th House), the ghosts disperse. The Sun brings "Light" to the "Darkness." It exposes the secrets *safely* before they can destroy the native. It creates a solar boundary that death cannot cross.

3. **Wife's Protection:**

- *The Rule:* The wife must wear **Gold** (Jupiter) on her body constantly. Jupiter acts as a shield ("Guru's Protection") against the 8th House malice.

House 9: The Saffron Lady

(Venus in Sagittarius: The Pilgrim's Wealth)

The Architecture of the Mountain The 9th House is **Dhanu** (Sagittarius). It belongs to **Jupiter**. It is the House of **Dharma**,

Destiny (*Bhagya*), **Ancestors**, and **Long Travel**. When Venus enters here, she must change her clothes. She cannot be the Seductress. She cannot be the Merchant. She must become the **"Saffron Lady"**—the Devotee. Venus in the 9th is **Lakshmi sitting at the feet of Vishnu**. It is one of the most auspicious placements for wealth in the *Lal Kitab, provided* the native follows the strict rules of the house. The *Lal Kitab* says: **"Wealth comes through Hard Work and Dharma."**

The Dialogue: The Sweat of the Saint

Aruna: "The view here is magnificent, O Light. We are high on the mountain. The air is pure. I see a woman dressed in saffron robes, tending to a garden. She looks peaceful. She looks wealthy, but she works with her hands. Is this not the perfection of Venus?"

Surya: "It is perfection, Aruna, but it is **Hard-Earned**. The 9th House is the house of **Effort** (*Parishram*) leading to Destiny. Unlike the 2nd House (where wealth is inherited) or the 11th House (where wealth is gained through networks), the 9th House wealth comes from **Righteous Action**. Venus here promises that if the native works hard, the soil will turn to gold. But there is a catch. The 9th House is the home of **Jupiter**. Jupiter is the Monk. Venus is the Lover. If the native tries to enjoy 'Easy Luxury'—if he becomes lazy, or if he uses his wealth for immoral pleasures (alcohol/women)—Jupiter kicks Venus out. The *Lal Kitab* warns: **'If he stops working, the money stops flowing.'** He cannot retire. He must be the Saffron Lady who tends the garden every day. The moment he sits down, the garden withers."

The Parable of the Farmer King

- **The Passenger:** A man who builds his fortune from scratch. He may be in agriculture, publishing, or teaching (Jupiter/Venus fields).
- **The Virtue:** He is deeply respectful of his elders (Jupiter). He treats his wife with reverence. He works long hours,

even when he is rich. He does not delegate the core work.

- **The Reward:** His wealth grows like a Banyan tree—slowly, but unshakeably. His wife brings him luck ("Lady Luck"). His children are wise.
- **The Fall:** He decides he has enough money. He stops working. He starts drinking alcohol (Saturn/Rahu) and chasing women. He insults a priest or an elder.
- **The Crash:** The 9th House collapses. His "Luck" evaporates instantly. His ancestors turn their backs. He realizes too late that his wealth was a *salary* from God, not a gift.

The Remedial Logic: The Silver Square and the Neem Tree

To maintain the blessing of the Saffron Lady, we must honor the alliance of **Venus** and **Mars** (Action) under the roof of **Jupiter**.

1. **The Silver Square:**
   - *The Prescription:* Keep a **Square Piece of Silver** in the pocket or bury it under a Neem tree.
   - *The Alchemical Physics:*
     - **Silver** is **Moon** (Peace/Fluid).
     - **Square** is **Mars** (Effort/Courage).
     - **Neem Tree** is **Mars.**
     - Why Mars? Because the 9th House requires *Action.*
     - By burying the Silver Square under the Neem Tree, you are planting the "Seed of Peace" in the "Soil of Action." You are telling the Universe: "I am willing to work (Mars) for my peace (Moon/Venus)." It solidifies the fluid luck.
2. **Burying Silver in the Foundation:**
   - *The Prescription:* Bury a **Silver Brick** under the threshold of the house.
   - *The Physics:* This anchors the Venus energy. It prevents the "Lady Luck" from wandering away.
3. **The Red Cow:**
   - *The Prescription:* Serve a **Red Cow**.

- *The Physics:* Red is the color of the Sun/Mars (9th House energy). Cow is Venus. This harmonizes the Guest (Venus) with the Host (Sun/Jupiter).

Summary Of The Dangerous Beauty

Aruna looked back at the landscape of the Third Quadrant. He saw the Bronze Idol in the market, the Burning Chariot in the grave, and the Saffron Lady on the mountain.

Aruna: "The Third Quadrant is a test of character, Surya. In the **7th**, Venus tested our **Pride**. In the **8th**, Venus tested our **Integrity**. In the **9th**, Venus tested our **Diligence**."

Surya: "It is the test of **Maturity**, Charioteer. Desire must grow up. It starts as a selfish demand (7th). It becomes a dangerous secret (8th). It ends as a noble pursuit (9th). But the journey is not over. The Chariot must now climb to the frozen peaks of the **Final Quadrant**. Venus must enter the **House of Karma (10th)**. She must enter the **House of Profit (11th)**. And she must enter the **House of Moksha (12th)**. Prepare yourself. We are about to see what happens when the Goddess of Love meets the Lord of Discipline. Turn the page to **Chapter 11**."

CHAPTER 11: THE LUXURIOUS REST

(Venus in Houses 10, 11, and 12: The Final Quadrant)

The Ascent To The High Peaks

The Chariot groaned as it began the steep, treacherous ascent from the fertile valley of the 9th House. For the last leg of the journey, the horses had enjoyed the lush grass and the gentle incline of the "Saffron Lady." The air had been sweet with the scent of temple flowers, sandalwood, and righteous labor. Venus had found a temporary peace in the House of Dharma, where she served the Guru and tended the garden.

But now, the path narrowed dangerously.

The green vegetation thinned out, replaced by sharp, black volcanic rocks and veins of cold iron. The air grew thin, biting, and gray. The golden light of the Sun seemed to dim, filtered through a haze of frost. The warmth of the valley was a distant memory.

Aruna pulled his cloak tighter around his shoulders. The golden ornaments of the Chariot seemed to lose their luster in the harsh light of the upper atmosphere.

Aruna: "O Surya, the warmth is fading. The garden is far behind us. We are entering a land of stone and shadows. The wind howls like a hungry wolf. Why does Venus, the Goddess of Comfort, come to such a desolate place? Is this not the domain of Saturn?"

Surya: "She comes because the journey is not complete without **Duty** and **Release**, Aruna. We have entered the **Final Quadrant**. This is the **Zone of Karma and Moksha**. In the **10th House**, Venus enters the **Fortress of Saturn**. Here, the Lover must become the Worker. She faces a wall of clay that blocks her vision. She must learn that Love is not just a feeling; it is a Structure. In the **11th House**, she enters the **Court of Profit**. Here, luxury becomes oil—slippery, flammable, and essential for the machine. In the **12th House**, she reaches the **Bed of Roses**. This is her exaltation. This is where Desire dissolves into Sleep. But the path to the bed is treacherous. In the 10th, Venus can blind the wife. In the 11th, she can turn wealth into sin. In the 12th, she can turn the wife into a shadow. Tighten your grip, Charioteer. We are about to see if Love can survive in the thin air of Destiny."

House 10: The Wall Of Clay

(Venus in Capricorn: The Blind Wife)

The Architecture of the Fortress The 10th House is **Karma Sthan** (House of Action). It is the Zenith—the highest point in the sky at noon. It belongs to **Saturn** (Capricorn). It is the house of Government, Career, the Father's status, the Bones, and the hard reality of the world. Saturn is cold, hard, and dry. Venus is warm, soft, and moist. When Venus enters here, she is **"The Flower in the Stone."** She is uncomfortable. She wants to play, but Saturn demands work. She wants to love, but Saturn demands duty. The *Lal Kitab* gives a specific and strange warning for this placement: **"The Wall of Clay"** (*Kachcha Deewar*). It says that Venus in the 10th acts like a mud wall that blocks the view. It blinds the native to the reality of his own home. Specifically, it creates health issues for the **Wife**.

The Dialogue: The Queen in the Factory

Aruna: "I see a beautiful woman standing in a noisy factory. Her silk dress is stained with soot. She looks exhausted. Why is she here?"

Surya: "She is here to learn **Architecture**, Aruna. But the lesson is harsh. The 10th House (Career) looks directly at the **4th House** (Home). When Venus sits in the 10th, she casts her gaze on the 4th. But Saturn (the Landlord of the 10th) dislikes Venus interfering in his work. He sees her as a distraction. The result is a conflict between **Ambition** and **Affection**. The native becomes so obsessed with his career (10th) that he treats his wife (Venus) like an employee. Or, his wife becomes sickly because the 'Cold

Air' of Saturn freezes her 'Fluid' nature. The *Lal Kitab* says: **'The wife will have eye trouble or problems with her reproductive organs.'** She becomes the casualty of his ambition. She absorbs the stress of his work."

The Parable of the Architect's Wife

- **The Passenger:** A successful architect, builder, or government official (Saturn/Venus professions). He is a workaholic. He builds palaces for others. He is respected in society.
- **The Shadow:** His own home is cold. His wife feels neglected. She develops chronic health issues—ovarian cysts, weak eyesight, or depression.
- **The Clay Wall:** He is "blind" to her suffering. He thinks providing money is enough. He has built a "Wall of Clay" between his heart and his duty. He cannot see the ruin of his own house because he is too busy looking at the blueprint of his career.
- **The Crisis:** Just as he reaches the peak of his career, his wife falls seriously ill. The medical bills drain the wealth he worked so hard to build. The Saturn-Venus conflict manifests as "Wealth vs. Health."

The Remedial Logic: The Mud Wall (Kachcha Deewar)

To save the wife and harmonize the energy, we must physically enact the metaphor of the "Wall." We must build it so we can destroy it.

1. **The Mud Wall Ritual:**
   - *The Prescription:* The native should build a **Mud Wall** (*Kachcha Deewar*) somewhere in his house (even a small symbolic one in the garden) and then destroy it.
   - *The Alchemical Physics:*
     - **Mud/Clay** represents **Venus** (Earth) mixed with **Saturn** (Structure).
     - The "Wall" represents the blockage in the 10th

House.
  - By physically building it, you acknowledge the planetary geometry. By destroying it, you ritually "break" the blockage.
  - You are telling the Universe: "I have removed the barrier between my Career (10th) and my Home (4th). I have opened the view."

2. **West Wall Construction:**
  - *The Prescription:* Ensure the West wall of the house (Saturn's direction) is strong and has no windows.
  - *The Physics:* This contains the Saturn energy so it doesn't leak out and attack the Venus energy. It keeps the "Cold Wind" out.
3. **Donate Almonds:**
  - *The Prescription:* Donate almonds (Saturn) to a temple.
  - *The Physics:* This appeases the Landlord (Saturn) so he stops harassing the Tenant (Venus). It pays the rent.

House 11: The Oil Of Luxury

(Venus in Aquarius: The Slippery Profit)

The Architecture of the Profit Zone The 11th House is **Labh Sthan** (House of Gains). It belongs to **Saturn** (Aquarius) and **Jupiter**. It is the house of Social Networks, Elder Siblings, Ambition, and the fulfillment of desires. Here, Venus is in the house of her friend, Saturn. On the surface, this looks excellent. Venus (Luxury) + 11th House (Gain) = **Luxury Gain**. The native often makes money through female friends, fashion, cinema, or liquid commodities (Oil). But the *Lal Kitab* warns: **"Oil is slippery."** The wealth here is volatile. It changes shape. And it demands a specific fuel to keep burning.

The Dialogue: The Lamp and the Oil

Aruna: "This looks like a banquet hall, Surya. Gold cups, fine wine, laughter. Surely the Goddess is happy here?"

Surya: "She is happy, Aruna, but she is **Restless**. In the 11th House, Venus becomes **The Socialite**. The native seeks pleasure in groups. He wants to be seen. He measures his worth by the applause of the crowd. But remember the chemistry: **Saturn + Venus = Oil.** The wealth of this native is like oil. It fuels the lamp of his life. But if he becomes greedy—if he tries to hoard the oil —it becomes stagnant and rancid. And there is a secret danger. The 11th House looks at the **5th House** (Children). If Venus is afflicted here (e.g., by Mercury), the native's 'social life' destroys his 'progeny.' He spends so much time chasing the world that he neglects his own blood. The *Lal Kitab* says: **'He changes his friends like he changes his clothes.'** His loyalty is fluid."

The Parable of the Oil Tycoon

- **The Passenger:** A man who trades in liquids—oil, chemicals, or perfumes. He is wealthy and popular. He throws the best parties.
- **The Flaw:** He is addicted to the "High Life." He spends lavishly on appearances. He believes his luck will never run out. He ignores his children.
- **The Slide:** Suddenly, a shipment is lost. A friend betrays him. His wealth slips through his fingers like oil. He realizes he has no real foundation.
- **The Cause:** He stopped "lubricating" the machine of destiny. He stopped donating. He thought the oil was for him alone.

The Remedial Logic: The Mustard Oil Offering

To stabilize the wealth, we must return the "Oil" to its source (Saturn). We must grease the gears of Karma.

1. **The Oil Donation (Shani Daan):**
   - *The Prescription:* Donate **Mustard Oil** on Saturdays. Pour the oil into a bowl, look at your reflection in it (*Chhaya Daan*), and give it to a beggar or temple.
   - *The Alchemical Physics:*

- **Mustard Oil** represents **Saturn** in liquid form (Venus aspect).
- By looking at your reflection, you transfer your "Karma" into the oil.
- By donating it, you "lubricate" the gears of the 11th House. You prevent the wealth from becoming "Sticky" (Attachment) or "Slippery" (Loss). You ensure the machine runs smoothly.

2. **Cotton Wicks:**

- *The Prescription:* Use cotton wicks dipped in oil to light lamps in the house.
- *The Physics:*
  - **Cotton** is **Venus.**
  - **Oil** is **Saturn.**
  - **Fire** is **Mars/Sun.**
  - Lighting the lamp integrates the energies of the chart. It turns the "Dark Oil" of Saturn into "Light." It transforms heavy wealth into spiritual illumination.

3. **Respect the Elder Brother:**

- *The Rule:* The native must maintain good relations with elder siblings (11th House karaka). If he fights with them, Venus turns against him.

House 12: The Bed Of Roses

(Venus in Pisces: The Exalted Sleeper)

The Architecture of the Bedroom The 12th House is **Vyaya Sthan** (House of Loss/Expense). It belongs to **Jupiter** (Pisces) and **Rahu** (The Void). It represents Sleep, Dreams, Foreign Lands, Hospitals, and the **Bedroom Pleasure** (*Shayya Sukh*). Here, Venus is **Exalted** (*Ucca*). This is the highest dignity of Venus. Why is the Goddess of Materialism exalted in the House of Loss? Because the ultimate luxury is **Rest**. The ultimate pleasure is **Surrender**.

The *Lal Kitab* calls this placement **"The Bed of Roses."** The native is destined for comfort. Even if he is poor, he will sleep on a soft mattress.

The Dialogue: The Dream of the Goddess

Aruna: "The Chariot has stopped, O Light. We are in a room filled with silken curtains and soft light. The air smells of roses. The Goddess is asleep. Is this the end of the journey?"

Surya: "It is the end of **Struggle**, Aruna. In the 12th House, Venus does not need to work (6th) or trade (7th). She simply *is*. This native is a magnet for luxury. Comfort finds him. If he travels, he gets upgraded. If he falls, he lands on a cushion. However, there is a price for this exaltation. The 12th House is the house of **Donation**. If the native tries to be miserly—if he refuses to spend money on others—the Bed of Roses develops thorns. His wife (Venus) may become the **'Blue Flower'** (Rahu)—beautiful but illusory. She may act as a drain on his resources, or she may be spiritual and detached."

The Parable of the Sleeping Prince

- **The Passenger:** A man who seems to lack ambition but lives well. He may live off investments or a spouse's wealth. He loves art, poetry, and sleep. He hates confrontation.
- **The Blessing:** He has a "Golden Touch" when it comes to spending. When he spends money, it comes back multiplied.
- **The Wife:** His wife is his savior. She shields him from the harshness of the world. She is the "Exalted Venus."
- **The Danger: The Blue Flower.**
  - If Rahu afflicts this Venus, the wife becomes sickly or secretive. The "Bed" becomes a place of illness (Hospital) rather than pleasure.
  - The native may suffer from **Insomnia** despite the soft bed.

The Remedial Logic: The Wife's Charity

To maintain the Exalted status, the native must empower the "Living Venus" (The Wife) to control the Demon (Rahu).

1. **The Wife's Donation:**
   - *The Prescription:* The native's wife should bury a **Blue Flower** or a **Blue Stone** in the earth.
   - *The Alchemical Physics:*
     - **Blue** is **Rahu.**
     - **Earth** is **Venus.**
     - The 12th House is co-ruled by Rahu (The Void). Rahu tries to destabilize the Exalted Venus.
     - By having the *Wife* (Venus) bury the Blue Flower (Rahu), she symbolically conquers the demon. She grounds the illusion. She clears the "Smoke" from the bedroom.
2. **The Cow Charity:**
   - *The Prescription:* The wife should donate a **Cow** (or cow-equivalent charity like fodder) using her own hands.
   - *The Physics:* This solidifies the Venus energy as "Dharma" (Jupiter/12th House) rather than just "Pleasure."
3. **Respect the Bed:**
   - *The Rule:* The native must keep his bedroom immaculate. No eating in bed. No clutter under the bed.
   - *The Logic:* The Bed is the altar of the 12th House Venus. Disrespecting it (Rahu/Dirt) insults the Goddess.

Summary Of The Luxurious Rest

Aruna lowered the reins. The horses bowed their heads, exhausted but calm. They had traversed the Stone Fortress, the Slippery Court, and the Silken Chamber.

Aruna: "The journey of Desire ends in Sleep, Surya. In the **10th**, Venus learned that Love requires a Wall to protect it. In the

11th, Venus learned that Wealth requires Oil to flow. In the **12th**, Venus learned that Luxury is a form of Prayer."

Surya: "You have mastered the Garden, Charioteer. You have seen the Seed (1st), the Fruit (2nd), the Flower (5th), and the Perfume (12th). The Chariot is now balanced. We have the **Engine** (Sun). We have the **Coolant** (Moon). We have the **Fuel** (Venus).

PART IV: THE ALCHEMY OF ASSOCIATION

(The Science of Planetary Conjunctions)

CHAPTER 12: THE MOON'S ALLIANCES

(The Fluid Mixtures: Moon + Sun, Moon + Mars, Moon + Jupiter)

The Convergence Of Horses

The Chariot slowed as it reached a high, windswept plateau. Behind them lay the twelve cities of the Zodiac—the twelve houses where the Moon and Venus had lived, suffered, and triumphed in solitude. Aruna looked back at the winding road. He saw the solitary figure of the Moon ruling the 4th House like a lonely Queen, and the isolated Venus sleeping in the 12th House like a dreaming Princess.

But as he looked forward, the nature of the path changed fundamentally.

The separate tracks on the cosmic road began to merge. The planets were no longer standing in their own castles, isolated by walls of stone and silence. They were gathering in the open fields of destiny. He saw the Sun walking beside the Moon, their hands clasped. He saw Mars riding on the back of Venus, their energies entwined. He saw Jupiter holding hands with Rahu, the Guru guiding the Demon. The sky was filled with strange, hybrid colors—purples born of red and blue, greens born of yellow and blue.

Aruna felt a shift in the air pressure. The simplicity of the single note was gone; the air now vibrated with chords, some harmonious, some dissonant.

Aruna: "O Surya, the geometry of the heavens is changing. Until now, we have studied the planets in isolation. We asked: 'What does the Moon do in the 1st House?' or 'What does Venus do in the 7th?' But now, I see them colliding. I see two, sometimes three planets occupying the same room, eating from the same plate. What happens when the King (Sun) sits on the same throne as the Mother (Moon)? Do they fight for dominance? Do they merge into a single being? Or do they cancel each other out, leaving a void?"

Surya: "We have entered the **Fourth Stage** of knowledge, Aruna. This is **The Alchemy of Association** (*Yuti*). In the *Lal Kitab*, the mathematics of the universe changes here. In this realm, **1 + 1 does not equal 2.** Think of a painter's palette. When you mix Blue and Yellow paint, you do not get 'Blue and Yellow' standing side by side. You get **Green**. You get a third, entirely new color that has properties of neither parent. Green is not the sky (Blue), nor is it the sun (Yellow); it is the grass. When you mix Fire and Water, you do not get wet fire; you get **Steam**—a force capable of moving mountains and driving engines. This is the secret of **Masnui Grah** (Artificial Planets). When two planets sit together in a house, they cease to be themselves. They surrender their individual egos to become a compound element. They create a 'Third Force.' We must now learn the chemistry of these mixtures. We must learn to predict the properties of the alloy, not just the base metals. We begin with the **Moon**—the Mind. The Mind is water. It has no color, no shape, and no taste of its own. It takes the color of whatever is dropped into it. If you drop Gold (Jupiter) into it, it becomes Holy Water, capable of purifying sins. If you drop Red Clay (Mars) into it, it becomes Mud, capable of building or blinding. If you drop Poison (Saturn) into it, it becomes Death. Let us examine the **Benefic Alliances**—the mixtures that create life, wealth, and power."

The Harvest: Moon + Sun

(The Combination of Parents: The Pious Wealth)

The Chemistry of the New Moon In traditional Vedic astrology, when the Moon sits with the Sun, it is called **Amavasya** (New Moon). The Moon is dark. It is considered weak because it has no light of its own. It is burnt by the Sun's proximity, rendered invisible in the sky. Astrologers often fear this conjunction, predicting a weak mind or a short life. But the *Lal Kitab* sees this differently. It looks beyond the astronomy to the **Social Reality**

and the **Alchemical Potential**. The Sun is the **Father** (*Pita*). He represents the Soul, the Bone, the Government, and the Law. The Moon is the **Mother** (*Mata*). She represents the Mind, the Blood, the Home, and the Mercy. When the Father and Mother sit together in the same house, the result is not darkness; it is **Unity**. It is the "Unified Family." It represents a home where the parents are together, supporting each other, presenting a united front to the world. The resulting energy is **"The Marble Stone"** or **"The Pious Wealth."**

The Dialogue: The Meeting of Day and Night

Aruna: "I see the Sun and Moon standing together in the 1st House. The glare of the Sun is blinding, and the Moon is invisible to the naked eye. Is the Mind not burnt by the Soul? Does the King not silence the Queen with his overwhelming presence?"

Surya: "The Mind is not burnt, Aruna; it is **Illuminated**. When the Moon merges with the Sun, the native loses his 'fickle' nature. The Moon usually waxes and wanes; it is unstable, emotional, and prone to changing its mind. But the Sun is constant. The Sun never changes its shape. When they join, the fluctuating tides of the Moon are stabilized by the gravity of the Sun. This native is a **Pious Rich Man**. He does not chase money with frantic energy; money chases him. He possesses a quiet authority. But there is a condition—a strict karmic clause. The Moon + Sun combination acts like a **Harvest**. If the native maintains his character (Sun) and his peace (Moon), the harvest is golden. But if he insults the Sun (Father) or the Moon (Mother)—if he separates his parents, creates discord between them, or disrespects their memory—the combination turns into a Solar Eclipse. The Marble cracks, and the structure of his life collapses."

The Parable of the Quiet Emperor

- **The Passenger:** A man who inherits a family business or rises to a high government position. He is known for his calm demeanor. He never shouts, never panics, and never gloats. He wears white or saffron.

- **The Alchemy:** His decisions (Sun) are always tempered by empathy (Moon). He does not rule with an iron fist, nor does he rule with a bleeding heart. His emotions (Moon) are always guided by duty (Sun). He is the perfect administrator. When he speaks, people listen, not out of fear, but out of respect for his balance.
- **The Danger: The 10th House Conflict.**
    - If Sun + Moon sit together in the **10th House** (Saturn's House), the mixture fails catastrophically.
    - *The Physics:* The Sun (Fire) melts Saturn's ice. The Moon (Water) freezes in the dark. The result is a chaotic slush. The native is misunderstood, faces government penalties, and often suffers from severe eye trouble (Sun/Moon conflict). The "Unified Family" cannot survive in the "Court of the Enemy."
- **The Remedy:** To stabilize this conjunction, the native must honor the connection between the Luminaries.
    - *Ritual:* Throwing a **Copper Coin** (Sun) into a **River** (Moon). This strengthens the bond. It tells the Universe: "I honor the King in the Queen's domain." It harmonizes the Fire and Water.

The Wealth Of Blood: Moon + Mars

(Chandra-Mangal Yoga: The Steam Engine)

The Chemistry of the Boiling Pot Mars is **Fire** (*Agni*). It is red, hot, aggressive, and rules the blood, the marrow, and the weapon. Moon is **Water** (*Jal*). It is cool, white, passive, and rules the plasma, the sap, and the nurturance. When Mars and Moon sit together, the Water boils. This creates **Steam**. Steam is powerful. It drives engines. It creates motion. It is dynamic. In the *Lal Kitab*, this combination is known as **"The Wealth of Blood"** or **"The Unstoppable Merchant."** It represents intense ambition, emotional drive, and the ability to monetize passion. It is the alchemy of the "Hot Mind."

The Dialogue: The Red River

Aruna: "This mixture is volatile, O Light. The water is bubbling furiously. Steam is rising, turning the wheels of a great machine. Is this dangerous? Can the vessel hold such pressure without exploding?"

Surya: "It is **Power**, Aruna. A pot of cold water sits still. A pot of boiling water can drive a locomotive across a continent. The Native with Moon + Mars is a dynamo. He cannot sit still. He sleeps little. His mind is always racing, plotting, conquering. He has the **Moon's Intuition** backed by **Mars's Courage**. He is the perfect businessman. He smells profit (Moon) and hunts it down (Mars). He does not wait for opportunity; he creates it. However, this combination has a dark side. Mars is 'Blood.' Moon is 'Liquid.' This native often earns money through **pain**, **conflict**, or **crisis**. He may be a surgeon (who cuts to heal), a soldier, a weapons dealer, or a ruthless trader who profits when others panic. If the Moon is weak, the 'Water' dries up, and the 'Fire' burns the vessel. The native becomes angry, abusive to his mother, and mentally unstable. The steam explodes, scalding everyone nearby."

The Parable of the Restless Warrior

- **The Passenger:** A self-made entrepreneur. He started with nothing but a dream and a temper. He fights for every coin. He treats business like war. He is protective but aggressive.
- **The Strength:** He is fiercely protective of his family (Moon). He will kill (Mars) to protect his mother. His love is intense and active.
- **The Flaw:** He lacks patience. If he doesn't get what he wants instantly, he boils over. He suffers from high blood pressure (Boiling Blood) and insomnia. He cannot relax because relaxation feels like death to him.
- **The Test of Character:** The *Lal Kitab* warns: **"Do not sell your integrity for gold."**

- Because this yoga generates so much wealth, the native is tempted to use illegal means (Mars negative). If he does, the steam explodes, causing accidents, blood disorders, or the sudden loss of the mother.

The Remedial Logic: The Silver Pot

To manage the steam, we must cool the container without extinguishing the fire. We need a strong vessel that can withstand the heat.

1. **The Silver Container:**
   - *The Prescription:* Keep water in a **Silver Pot** (or a glass with a silver coin in it) in the house.
   - *The Alchemy:* **Silver** is Pure Moon. It thickens the walls of the vessel. It allows the Mars energy to heat the water without melting the pot. It converts "Rage" into "Productivity." It provides a cooling buffer for the aggression.
2. **Sweet Water Distribution:**
   - *The Prescription:* Offer **Sweet Water** (Sherbat) to people, especially during the day.
   - *The Physics:* Sugar is Mars (Energy). Water is Moon (Cooling). Sharing this mixture harmonizes the energy socially. It releases the pressure valve. It transforms the "Boiling Blood" into "Nectar" for others.

The Gaj Kesari: Moon + Jupiter

(The Gold and the Water: The Banyan Tree)

The Chemistry of the Holy Water Jupiter is **Air/Ether** (*Guru*). It is Wisdom, Expansion, Gold, the Breath, and the Teacher. Moon is **Water** (*Mind*). When they combine, it is the most auspicious mixture in the *Lal Kitab*. It is **"Ganga Jal"** (Holy Water). It is **"The Banyan Tree near the Well."** The Banyan (Jupiter) provides shade, oxygen, and deep roots. The Well (Moon) provides nourishment and sustenance. The tree protects the water from the sun, and the water feeds the tree. They exist in perfect symbiosis. This combination creates a native who is wise, wealthy, and fundamentally peaceful.

The Dialogue: The Tree of Life

Aruna: "The turbulence has ceased, Surya. I see a giant tree with golden leaves growing by a clear, flowing river. The shade is cool. The water is sweet. This feels like the ultimate refuge. Is there any flaw here? Is there any danger?"

Surya: "It is the **Gaj Kesari**, Aruna—the Elephant (Jupiter) and the Lion (Moon/Mars aspect). But in our Red Book, we call it **The Teacher's Wealth**. When Wisdom (Jupiter) guides the Mind (Moon), the result is **Unshakeable Reputation**. This native may not have the burning ambition of the Moon+Mars merchant, but he has something more valuable: **Trust**. People trust him with their lives, their secrets, and their money. He succeeds in education, counseling, banking, or ministry. Even if he is born in a slum, he will die in a palace, because his 'Good Karma' (Jupiter) constantly refills his 'Bank' (Moon). He is the source of water for others. He is the Banyan Tree that shelters the village. But yes, there is one danger. **Hypocrisy.**"

Aruna: "Hypocrisy?"

Surya: "Jupiter is the Guru. If this native uses his wisdom to deceive—if he pretends to be a Guru to steal money, or if he uses his reputation to harm others—Jupiter turns into a Judge. The Gold turns to lead, and the Water turns to poison. He loses his reputation, which is his true wealth. The Banyan tree rots from the inside."

The Parable of the Wise Banker

- **The Passenger:** A teacher, a consultant, or a spiritual leader. He speaks slowly. He listens more than he talks. He is often the unofficial judge of his community. People come to him to settle disputes.

- **The Destiny:** Money flows to him effortlessly, but he is not attached to it. He uses it to build schools, temples, or libraries. He understands that wealth is a tool for Dharma.
- **The Protection:** The *Lal Kitab* says: **"Jupiter protects the Moon like a father protects a daughter."**
  - Even in the worst planetary periods (Dasha of Rahu), this native is safe. The "Gold" purifies the "Water." If he falls, a cushion appears. If he is attacked, a defender arises.
- **The Karmic Law:** He must never disrespect a teacher or a priest. If he does, the protective shield shatters.

The Remedial Logic: The Saffron Spot

To maintain the sanctity of this alliance, the native must honor the Guru.

1. **The Kesar Tilak:**
   - *The Prescription:* Apply **Saffron** (Kesar) on the forehead daily.
   - *The Alchemy:*
     - Saffron is **Jupiter**.
     - The Forehead is the seat of the Mind (**Moon/ Mercury**).
     - By applying Jupiter to the Mind, you ensure the connection remains active. You permit Wisdom to rule Emotion. You crown the Mind with Gold. You remind the self that it is guided by something higher.
2. **Respect the Grandfather:**
   - *The Prescription:* Serve the grandfather, elderly priests, or teachers.
   - *The Physics:* They are the living embodiments of Jupiter. Serving them waters the roots of the Banyan Tree. It keeps the flow of "Ganga Jal" pure.

Summary Of The Moon's Alliances

Aruna looked at the three combinations swirling in the cosmic mixing bowl. The radiant Pious Man (Sun+Moon), the boiling Warrior (Mars+Moon), and the serene Guru (Jupiter+Moon).

Aruna: "The Moon is a chameleon, Surya. With the Sun, she becomes **Light**. With Mars, she becomes **Fuel**. With Jupiter, she becomes **Wisdom**."

Surya: "The Mind has no shape, Charioteer. It becomes what it touches. These were the **Friends**. When the Moon meets her friends, she creates civilization. She creates Wealth, Power, and Dharma. But what happens when the Moon meets her **Enemies**? What happens when the Water meets the **Poison of Saturn**? What happens when the Mind meets the **Confusion of Ketu**? What happens when Logic (Mercury) tries to dissect Emotion? Prepare yourself. The road ahead is dark. The sky is turning grey. We must now enter the **Toxic Mixtures**. We must learn how to handle the **Moon's Poisons**. Turn the page to **Chapter 13**."

CHAPTER 13: THE MOON'S POISONS

(The Toxic Mixtures: Moon + Saturn, Moon + Mercury, Moon + Ketu)

The Darkening Of The Waters

The Chariot shuddered violently as it crossed the invisible boundary into the darker hemisphere of the Zodiac. Behind them lay the golden fields of the "Harvest" (Sun + Moon) and the lush forests of the "Banyan Tree" (Jupiter + Moon). The air there had been sweet, filled with the hum of bees and the scent of ripening fruit—the aroma of a life lived in harmony.

But now, the light failed.

The clear, golden light of the Sun faded into a bruised purple twilight. The steam of the Mars-Moon engine cooled into a thick, clinging gray fog that smelled of sulfur, old copper, and stagnant water. The protective shade of the Jupiter-Moon Banyan tree withered, its leaves turning black and falling away, leaving the road exposed to a biting, whistling wind.

Aruna pulled his cloak tighter around his shoulders. The horses were nervous, their ears twitching at sounds he could not hear—whispers from the shadows, the slither of scales on stone, the scratching of dry leaves.

Aruna: "O Surya, the light is failing. The air smells of decay. We have left the company of friends. Who are these shadows gathering at the edge of the road? Why does the Moon look so pale, so fragile? She seems to be trembling, like a reflection in disturbed water."

Surya: "We have entered the **Zone of Toxicity**, Aruna. The Moon is the Mind. It is delicate. It is impressionable. It has no light of its own; it only reflects what is around it. When the Moon meets her friends (Sun, Mars, Jupiter), she thrives. She becomes a Queen, a Warrior, a Guru. She takes on their strength. But now, she must meet her **Enemies**. She must meet **Saturn** (The Poison). She must meet **Mercury** (The Critic). She must meet **Ketu** (The Eclipse). In these conjunctions, the 'Water' of peace is not boiled or purified; it is polluted. It is contaminated at the source. Moon + Saturn creates **Ink**—dark, permanent, and staining. It turns the water black. Moon + Mercury creates **Foam**—agitated, useless motion. It turns the water into a storm. Moon + Ketu creates **Vacuum**—an emptiness that sucks the soul dry. It drains the water into the void. Tighten your grip, Charioteer. We are about to learn how to drive a Chariot when the driver is blind, deaf, or mad."

The Vish Yoga: Moon + Saturn

(The Poison Combination: The Blind Horse)

The Chemistry of Ink Saturn is **Darkness**, **Iron**, **Oil**, **Ice**, and **Snake Poison**. He represents the heavy weight of Karma, the cold reality of death, the slow grind of time, and the judgment of history. He is the colour Black. Moon is **Light**, **Silver**, **Water**, **Milk**, and **Emotion**. She represents the flight of fancy, the need for comfort, the nurturing instinct, and the present moment. She is the colour White.

When you mix Milk and Poison, you do not get diluted poison; you get **Death**. This combination is known in Vedic Astrology as **Vish Yoga** (Poison Yoga). In the *Lal Kitab*, it is called **"The Ink in the Milk"** or **"The Blind Horse."**

Imagine a beautiful white horse (Moon) that has been blinded. It has energy, it has strength, but it has no direction. It runs in circles, terrified of the dark, crashing into walls. It cannot see the path, only the shadows. Or imagine a single drop of black ink falling into a glass of pure white milk. The milk does not turn gray; it turns ruined. You cannot drink it. It becomes toxic. This combination represents a mind that has been stained by **Pessimism**.

The Dialogue: The Weight of the Past

Aruna: "I see a man carrying a heavy stone on his chest. He is weeping, but he does not put the stone down. In fact, he clutches it tighter, as if it were a child. Why does he suffer so? Why does he not release the weight?"

Surya: "Because he believes the stone is part of him, Aruna. When Saturn (The Past/Karma) sits with the Moon (The Present Mind), the native cannot let go. This is the placement of **Depression**, **Chronic Fear**, and **Melancholy**. The native sees the glass not just as half-empty, but as cracked and leaking poison. His memories are not sources of joy; they are prisons. He remembers every insult, every failure, every loss. He replays them in the cinema of his mind until they define him. And the poison seeps into his life structure. If he builds a house (Saturn domain), his mother (Moon domain) falls ill. If he buys a vehicle (Moon domain), it meets with an accident (Saturn domain). The two energies are chemically incompatible. Saturn freezes the Moon. The mind becomes a glacier—slow, cold, and crushing. He moves, but he does not live. He survives, but he does not thrive."

The Parable of the Architect of Sorrow

- **The Passenger:** A talented builder, engineer, or administrator (Saturn professions). He is hardworking, serious, and dressed in drab colors—greys, browns, blacks. He rarely smiles. He is efficient but joyless.
- **The Mind:** He wakes up tired. He goes to sleep worried. He replays old conversations in his head like a broken record, finding new ways to blame himself for things that happened years ago. He feels responsible for the sins of the world. He anticipates disaster before it arrives.
- **The Mother's Curse:** His mother suffered greatly during his childhood, or she was emotionally cold, distant, or depressed. The "Source" of his water was frozen at the root. He learned early that love is painful, that needs are burdens.
- **The Crisis:** He accumulates wealth (Saturn), but he cannot enjoy it (Moon). He lives like a pauper in a palace. He hoards money for a "rainy day" that never ends. He fears that if he

smiles, the gods will notice him and punish him. He is the Architect of his own Sorrow.

The Remedial Logic: Feeding the Snakes

To separate the Poison from the Milk, we must appease the Source of the Poison (Saturn/Rahu). We must externalize the toxin so it doesn't consume the host.

1. **Feeding Snakes (Nag Sewa):**
   - *The Prescription:* Offer milk to snakes (or pour milk on a Shiva Lingam/Snake Idol) on Saturdays or Nag Panchami.
   - *The Alchemical Physics:*
     - Saturn governs **Snakes** and **Poison.**
     - By voluntarily offering the "Moon" (Milk) to the "Saturn" (Snake) in a ritual context, you are paying the "Ransom."
     - You are telling the Snake: "Take this offering and leave my mind alone. Drink this milk, not my blood."
     - This externalizes the poison. Instead of the poison being inside the mind (Depression), it is transferred to the ritual object. The Snake drinks the "Moon," leaving the "Mind" clear.
2. **The Oil Vessel (Chhaya Daan):**
   - *The Prescription:* Keep **Mustard Oil** in a glass bottle and sink it into a river or pond.
   - *The Alchemical Physics:*
     - Oil is **Saturn**. Water is **Moon.**
     - Usually, oil floats on water (separation/irritation). But sinking the container forces the Saturn energy to be "swallowed" by the Moon's vastness (River) safely.
     - The River washes the oil away. It dissolves the heavy karma in the flow of time. It tells the subconscious that the burden has been lifted and car-

ried away by the current.

3. **Do Not Drink Milk at Night:**
   - *The Law:* **Absolute Prohibition.**
   - *The Logic:* Night is **Saturn**. Milk is **Moon**. Drinking milk at night physically enacts the Vish Yoga in the stomach. It creates toxins (*Ama*) and phlegm. It invites the darkness into the body. The native should drink milk only when the Sun is up.

The Poisoned Pot: Moon + Mercury

(The Suicide of the Mind: The Agitated Water)

The Chemistry of Foam Mercury is **Intellect, Logic, Speed, Communication**, and the **Parrot**. It is dry, airy, restless, and critical. It is the "Merchant." Moon is **Emotion, Peace, Silence**, and the **Heart**. It is the "Mother." In the *Lal Kitab*, **Mercury hates the Moon**. Why? Because Logic kills Emotion. You cannot "analyze" love; if you do, it dies. You cannot "calculate" peace. When Moon and Mercury sit together, it creates **"The Poisoned Pot."** Imagine a pot of water boiling not from fire, but from a violent chemical reaction. It froths. It hisses. It spills over. It generates steam but no power. It is **Mental Turbulence**. This is the combination of **Anxiety, Overthinking, Insomnia**, and **Suicidal Thoughts**.

The Dialogue: The Parrot and the Queen

Aruna: "I hear a voice that never stops talking. It argues, it calculates, it criticizes. The Moon tries to sleep, but the voice wakes her up. It mocks her tears. It dissects her dreams. Who is this tormentor?"

Surya: "It is the **Parrot**, Aruna. It is Mercury. The native with Moon + Mercury is brilliant but cursed. His mind is a racing engine with no brakes. He cannot differentiate between 'Feeling' and 'Thinking.' He analyzes his own happiness until it disappears. If someone smiles at him, Mercury asks: 'What do they want? What is their agenda?' If he succeeds, Mercury asks: 'When will I fail? How long will this last?' The *Lal Kitab* says: **'This native burns his own roof.'** He destroys his own peace. He is the **Drowning Swimmer**—he knows how to swim (Intellect), but when the wave comes, he panics (Emotion) and drowns because he tries to calculate the wave instead of floating on it."

The Parable of the Neurotic Genius

- **The Passenger:** A writer, a trader, a data analyst, or a media person. He is incredibly sharp. He notices details others miss. He speaks fast, his words tumbling over each other.
- **The Trap:** He has **Insomnia**. His brain refuses to shut down. He lies in bed planning conversations that will never happen, winning arguments in his head. He is prone to nervous breakdowns.
- **The Daughter:** Mercury represents the Daughter. Moon represents the Mother. Often, in this combination, the mother and daughter do not get along, or the daughter's birth brings a period of mental stress for the mother. The "Parrot" pecks at the "Queen."
- **The Danger:** If this combination is in the **4th House** (Moon's home) or **12th House** (Loss/Sleep), the risk of self-harm or deep clinical depression is high. The mind turns against itself, using its own intelligence as a weapon.

The Remedial Logic: The Alum (Phitkari) Cleaning

To save the water, we must stop the agitation. We need a coagulant to settle the dirt so the water becomes clear.

1. **The Alum Remedy:**
   - *The Prescription:* Clean the teeth with **Alum** (Phitkari) daily. Or, throw a piece of Alum into a drain.
   - *The Alchemical Physics:*
     - Alum is a chemical used to purify water. It makes the sediment settle to the bottom.
     - Mercury is the "Dirt" or "Sediment" clouding the

Moon water.

- Cleaning the teeth (Mercury rules teeth/mouth) with Alum neutralizes the "Acid speech" of Mercury. It settles the mind. It clears the foam. It stops the endless chatter.

2. **Feeding Young Girls:**
   - *The Prescription:* Give sweets and gifts to young girls (Kanyas).
   - *The Physics:* Young girls are the living avatars of **Mercury**. By serving them, you appease the enemy. You turn the "Critical Parrot" into a "Singing Bird." You make peace with the intellect.
3. **The Silver Glass:**
   - *The Prescription:* Always drink water from a **Silver Tumbler**.
   - *The Physics:* This strengthens the Moon. It gives the Water a "Moon-Metal" shield against the Mercury vibration.

The Eclipse: Moon + Ketu

(Grahan Yoga: The Vacuum)

The Chemistry of the Void Ketu is the **Tail of the Dragon**. It is **Detachment**, **Cutting**, **Smoke**, **Ash**, and the **Moksha-Karaka** (Significator of Liberation). Moon is **Attachment**, **Mind**, and **Comfort**. When Ketu sits with the Moon, it creates a **Lunar Eclipse** (*Chandra Grahan*). Ketu "swallows" the Moon. This is not the active poison of Saturn, nor the noisy agitation of Mercury. This is **Silence**. It is the **"Void in the Heart."** The native feels detached from the world. He may be surrounded by family, yet he feels like an orphan. He is present in the body, but absent in the spirit.

The Dialogue: The Monk in the House

Aruna: "This is the strangest of all, Surya. The Moon is there, but

I cannot feel her. It is as if she is behind a thick veil of smoke. The native looks at his children, but his eyes are looking at a distant mountain. Is he soulless?"

Surya: "He is not soulless; he is **Displaced**. Ketu is the planet of 'Letting Go.' Moon is 'Holding On.' When they combine, the native loses the ability to hold onto happiness. He earns money, but it disappears into thin air (Ketu). He loves his mother, but he is separated from her early, or she is sickly. The *Lal Kitab* calls this **'The Moon in the Ash Heap.'** But listen closely, Charioteer. This is also the combination of the **Mystic**. If the native channels this energy into spirituality, he becomes a Saint. He realizes the illusion of the world. But if he tries to live a worldly life, he becomes a Victim. He tries to grasp water, and it slips through his fingers."

The Parable of the Lost Son

- **The Passenger:** A man who wanders. He changes jobs, changes houses, changes beliefs. He has no roots (Ketu cuts roots). He is a drifter. He feels he doesn't belong anywhere.
- **The Mother:** His mother often suffers from joint pain, arthritis, or mysterious ailments (Ketu rules wind/pain). The "Moon" is being eaten by the "Termite" (Ketu).
- **The Psychology:** He suffers from a "phantom limb" pain in his soul. He misses a home he never had. He is easily manipulated because he lacks the "Ego-Shell" to protect himself. He is porous.

The Remedial Logic: The Golden Rod and the Dog

To fix the Eclipse, we must introduce the "Head" (Rahu) to balance the "Tail" (Ketu), or use "Gold" (Jupiter) to shield the Moon.

1. **The Golden Rod (Gold in Ear):**
   - *The Prescription:* Wear **Gold** in the ears.
   - *The Alchemical Physics:*
     - Gold is **Jupiter** (The Guru).
     - The Ear is the organ of **Ketu**.
     - By placing Jupiter (The Guru) in Ketu's house

(Ear), you control the Dragon's Tail. The Guru tames the wild energy of Ketu. It prevents Ketu from biting the Moon. It brings "Wisdom" to the "Void."

2. **Feeding Dogs:**
   - *The Prescription:* Feed stray dogs (especially two-colored or black/white dogs).
   - *The Physics:*
     - The Dog is the animal avatar of **Ketu**.
     - By feeding the Dog, you satisfy the hunger of the Eclipse. A fed dog guards the house; a hungry dog bites the owner. You turn the "Destroyer" into the "Protector."
3. **The Lemon Ritual:**
   - *The Prescription:* Float **Yellow Lemons** in a flowing river on a Sunday.
   - *The Physics:* The sourness of the lemon cuts the "Ash" of Ketu. The flowing river (Moon) carries the affliction away. It washes the ash from the face of the Moon.

Summary Of The Toxic Mixtures

Aruna looked at the three dark vials: The Ink (Saturn), the Foam (Mercury), and the Void (Ketu).

Aruna: "The Moon is fragile, Surya. With Saturn, she freezes into despair. With Mercury, she boils into anxiety. With Ketu, she vanishes into emptiness."

Surya: "The Mind is the most vulnerable part of the Chariot, Aruna. That is why it must be guarded so fiercely. The remedies —the Milk for Snakes, the Alum for Teeth, the Gold in the Ear —are not magic. They are **Chemical Stabilizers**. They prevent the Mind from exploding under the pressure of the Enemy. But we are not done with mixtures. We have seen the *Mind* under attack. Now we must see *Desire* under attack. What happens when **Venus** meets her energetic partners? What happens when Beauty meets the **Fire of Mars**? What happens when Beauty meets the **Smoke of Rahu**? Prepare yourself. We are entering the **Combustible Mixtures**. Turn the page to **Chapter 14**."

CHAPTER 14: THE VENUS MIXTURES

(The Combustible Alliances: Venus + Mars, Venus + Mercury, Venus + Rahu)

The Heat Of The Garden

The Chariot rattled violently as it tore itself away from the dark, cold gravity of the 13th Chapter. For the last leg of the journey, Aruna and Surya had navigated the "Zone of Toxicity," where the Moon was poisoned by Saturn's ink, agitated by Mercury's foam, and swallowed by Ketu's void. The air had been heavy with the stench of stagnant water and old sorrow.

But now, the wheels struck sparks against a new terrain.

The atmosphere shifted instantly. The biting cold vanished, replaced by a sudden, intense heat. The smell of decay was overpowered by a heavy, intoxicating perfume—a mix of crushed rose petals, burning sandalwood, musk, and the metallic tang of fresh blood. The silence of the void was shattered by the sound of laughter, the strumming of lyres, and the distant clash of swords.

Aruna loosened his grip on the reins. The horses, previously skittish and fearful, now pranced with a new, aggressive energy. Their eyes widened, reflecting the red and gold lights of the landscape ahead.

Aruna: "O Surya, the atmosphere has changed again. The heaviness is gone, but there is a new tension in the air. It is not the tension of fear, but of excitement. It feels dangerous, like a storm about to break. I see red flags flying from the palace walls. I see sparks flying from the wheels. What is this place?"

Surya: "We have left the **Zone of Mind** (Moon), Aruna. We have entered the **Zone of Desire** (Venus). The Moon was fragile; she needed protection. She was the Mother who hid her children from the storm. Venus is resilient; she demands expression. She is the Lover who dances in the rain. But Venus does not travel alone. She seeks partners. She is the planet of Union. And when she finds them, the chemistry is explosive. We must now examine the **Venus Mixtures**. What happens when Beauty meets the **Warrior** (Mars)? What happens when Beauty meets the **Prince** (Mercury)? What happens when Beauty meets the **Outlaw** (Rahu)? In these conjunctions, the 'Form' of life (Venus) meets the 'Force' of life. Venus + Mars creates **Fire**—passion that can build empires or burn them to the ground. Venus + Mercury creates **Light**—an artificial sun that dazzles the world with its brilliance. Venus + Rahu creates **Smoke**—a mesmerizing illusion that hides a core of base metal. Prepare yourself, Charioteer. These are the combinations that create the great lovers, the great artists, and the great scandals of history. The heat you feel is the heat of Life itself."

The Lover: Venus + Mars

(The Burning Passion: The Red Flower)

The Chemistry of Fire and Earth Venus is **Earth/Curd/Semen**. She is soft, yielding, beautiful, and receptive. She rules the skin, the art, and the pleasure of the senses. She is the capacity to enjoy. Mars is **Fire/Blood/Courage**. He is hard, aggressive, dominant, and rules the muscle, the marrow, and the weapon. He is the capacity to act. When Venus and Mars sit together in the same house, it is the meeting of the **Lover** and the **Warrior**. It creates a **High-Temperature Alloy**. In the *Lal Kitab*, this combination is not just about sex; it is about **Vitality**. It is the engine of creation. It is the steam that drives the piston. However, it is volatile. The *Lal Kitab* warns: **"If this fire is not contained, it burns the house."**

The Dialogue: The Sword and the Rose

Aruna: "I see a warrior holding a delicate flower. He protects it with his life, but his grip is so tight he might crush it. Is this love or possession? Is it creation or destruction?"

Surya: "It is **Passion**, Aruna. And passion always balances on the edge of destruction. The native with Venus + Mars has an immense zest for life. They are magnetic. They attract others like moths to a flame. They do not walk; they stride. They do not talk; they declare. They are not content with a quiet life. They want drama, intensity, and conquest. In a positive chart (e.g., in the 3rd House of Valor), this creates a **Creative Genius**—someone who can mold the world to their desire, an artist who paints with blood and fire. But in a negative chart (e.g., in the 7th House of Marriage), it creates a **Burning Temperament**. The native becomes jealous, possessive, and prone to 'Crimes of Passion.' The 'Blood' (Mars) boils the 'Semen' (Venus). This leads to blood disorders, skin rashes, or impulsive affairs that destroy families. The desire consumes the vessel."

The Parable of the Impulsive Artist

- **The Passenger:** A charismatic artist, actor, or soldier. He lives life in the fast lane. He falls in love instantly and deeply. He is the hero of his own movie. He buys expensive gifts he cannot afford.
- **The Conflict:** He cannot separate his anger from his love. When he fights with his wife, he breaks things. When he loves her, he smothers her. He equates intensity with intimacy. He believes that if it doesn't hurt, it isn't real.
- **The Crisis:** He develops a blood infection or a reproductive issue (Mars attacking Venus). His impulsive spending on luxury (Venus) leads to massive debt (Mars). He burns through his resources like a forest fire.
- **The Diagnosis:** The Fire is too hot for the Pot. The clay is cracking. The "Red Flower" is wilting in the heat.

The Remedial Logic: The Wet Clay

To cool the combination without killing the passion, we must introduce the **Moon** (Water) or **Saturn** (Earth/Cooling). We need to thicken the walls of the vessel so it can hold the heat.

1. **The Silver Square:**

- *The Prescription:* Keep a **Square Piece of Silver** in the pocket at all times.
- *The Alchemical Physics:*
  - **Silver** is **Moon** (The Coolant).
  - **Square** is **Mars** (The Structure).
  - By combining them, you create a "Cooled Structure" for the Mars energy. It prevents the Mars fire from burning the Venus beauty. It turns "Rage" into "Determination." It gives the fire a hearth to burn in safely.

2. **The Clay Pot (Budh):**
- *The Prescription:* Fill an earthen pot (*Matka*) with **Honey** (Mars) or **Desi Khand** (Sugar) and bury it in a deserted place.
- *The Physics:*
  - The Pot is **Mercury** (which cools Mars).
  - Honey is **Mars** (Sweet Mars).
  - Burying it "grounds" the excessive Mars energy. It stores the fire safely underground so it warms the house instead of burning it down. It satisfies the hunger of Mars.

The Artificial Sun: Venus + Mercury

(The Gandharva Yoga: The Eloquent Charmer)

The Chemistry of Light Venus is **Beauty/Lens/Form**. She is the Minister. Mercury is **Intellect/Light/Voice**. He is the Prince. When they combine, something magical happens. The *Lal Kitab* says: **"Venus and Mercury together create the Sun."** How? Because **Sun** is the King. **Mercury** is the Prince. **Venus** is the Minister. When the Prince and Minister agree, they rule with the authority of a King. They create a "Regency." This combination creates **"Artificial Sunlight"** (*Masnui Surya*). It represents **Charisma, Eloquence, Artistic Talent**, and **Social Grace**. The native shines. They are the center of attention. They do not need to be the King to rule the room; they rule through charm.

The Dialogue: The Mask of Gold

Aruna: "I see a figure wearing a golden mask. They speak, and everyone listens. They smile, and doors open. But is the light real? Is it the Sun? Or is it a reflection?"

Surya: "It is **Reflected Light**, Aruna. But it is powerful enough to rule. The native with Venus + Mercury is a master of **Presentation**. They know how to talk, how to dress, and how to sell. They succeed in media, marketing, diplomacy, or the arts. They are the Gandharvas—the celestial musicians. They have the 'Midas Touch'—whatever they touch turns to gold (Sun energy). However, there is a catch. This 'Artificial Sun' depends on **Harmony**. If Venus and Mercury fight (e.g., if the native cheats in business or uses their charm to deceive in love), the Sun vanishes. The mask falls off. The native is often accused of being superficial —'All style, no substance.' And physically, this combination can lead to **Nervous Exhaustion**. The nervous system (Mercury) is overstimulated by the pleasures of the senses (Venus). The wire burns out."

The Parable of the Golden Diplomat

- **The Passenger:** A successful PR agent, diplomat, or host. Their house is always full of guests. They are charming, witty, and impeccably dressed. They know exactly what to say to make people feel important.
- **The Power:** They can diffuse any argument with a smile. They make money effortlessly through connections. They sell ideas.
- **The Flaw:** They are terrified of being alone. They need an audience to exist. They lie to keep the peace. They promise more than they can deliver. They believe their own press.
- **The Fall:** If they become arrogant (False Sun), they suffer a public humiliation. The "Artificial Light" flickers and dies, leaving them in darkness.

The Remedial Logic: The Clean Mirror

To maintain the Artificial Sun, we must keep the components pure. We must polish the mirror.

1. **Cleaning the Teeth (Mercury):**
   - *The Prescription:* Use **Alum** (Phitkari) to clean teeth daily.
   - *The Physics:*
     - Mercury rules the **Teeth**.
     - Alum cleanses the "Sediment" and bacteria.
     - This keeps the Mercury energy sharp and clear, preventing it from clouding the Venus beauty. It ensures the "Voice" remains pure.
2. **The Cow and the Grass:**
   - *The Prescription:* Feed **Green Grass** to a **Cow**.
   - *The Alchemical Physics:*
     - **Green Grass** is **Mercury**.
     - **Cow** is **Venus**.
     - By feeding them together, you harmonize the two planets. You "feed" the Venus with Mercury. This ensures the "Artificial Sun" keeps burning brightly. It unites the Prince and the Minister.
3. **The Copper Coin:**
   - *The Prescription:* Wear a **Copper Coin** with a hole in it around the neck.
   - *The Physics:* Copper is **Sun**. By wearing the *actual* Sun metal, you stabilize the *Artificial* Sun energy. You give the "Mask" a real face. You anchor the charisma in authority.

The Bronze Alloy: Venus + Rahu

(The Scandalous Attraction: The Smoky Mirror)

The Chemistry of Illusion Venus is **Love/Materialism/Luxury**.

Rahu is **Obsession/Smoke/Expansion/The Foreign**. When they mix, they create a **High-Voltage Alloy**. The *Lal Kitab* calls this **"The Bronze Alloy"** (*Kansa*). Bronze is shiny, it looks like gold, but it is not Gold. It tarnishes. It rings with a different sound. This combination represents **Excessive Desire**, **Artificial Luxury**, and **Scandal**. It creates a native who is obsessed with the *image* of wealth and love. They want the "Instagram Life." They want the fantasy.

The Dialogue: The Mirage in the Desert

Aruna: "I see a palace that looks like gold, but when I touch it, it is cold metal. I see a lover who looks perfect, but their eyes are empty. What is this illusion? Why am I drawn to it?"

Surya: "It is **Maya**, Aruna. It is the Great Illusion. Venus + Rahu creates a native who is a master of **Glamour**. They are drawn to the film industry, fashion, or high-stakes gambling. They live in a world of filters. They have a magnetic sexual appeal that borders on the dangerous. But Rahu is 'Smoke.' He clouds the judgment of Venus. The native confuses 'Lust' with 'Love.' They confuse 'Expensive' with 'Valuable.' This leads to **Scandals**. The 'Secret Affairs' of the 8th House often stem from this combination. The native chases a mirage. They get the partner they want, only to realize they are empty inside. The *Lal Kitab* warns: **'The wife will suffer, or the native will suffer from the wife.'** The bronze will eventually turn black."

The Parable of the Fallen Star

- **The Passenger:** A movie star, a model, or a socialite. They are obsessed with beauty treatments and brands. They live for the applause.
- **The Trap:** They enter relationships that look perfect on paper but are toxic in reality. They attract partners who are deceptive (Rahu) or foreign to their culture. They marry for status, not love.
- **The Crash:** A sudden scandal destroys their reputation. Or,

they lose their wealth in a "Get Rich Quick" scheme (Rahu). The Bronze tarnishes. They realize they have built a castle on smoke.

The Remedial Logic: The Blue Flower

To separate the Venus from the Rahu, we must "Ground" the Rahu. We must pull the smoke out of the room.

1. **The Blue Flower Ritual:**
   - *The Prescription:* Bury a **Blue Flower** in the earth in a deserted place.
   - *The Alchemical Physics:*
     - **Blue** is **Rahu.**
     - **Earth** is **Venus.**
     - Why bury Rahu? Because Rahu is the "Smoke" that clouds the Venus mirror.
     - By burying the Blue Flower, you are trapping the Demon in the Earth. You are "grounding" the obsession. You are clearing the air so the true Venus can breathe.
2. **The Lead (Ranga) Bullet:**
   - *The Prescription:* Keep a piece of **Lead** (or a lead bullet) in the pocket.
   - *The Physics:* Lead is **Rahu**. By keeping it contained (in the pocket), you control the Rahu energy. You keep the "Smoke" in a bottle. You master the illusion instead of being mastered by it.
3. **Respect the In-Laws:**
   - *The Rule:* Maintain good relations with in-laws (Rahu/Ketu domain). This appeases the Nodes.

Summary Of The Combustible Mixtures

Aruna looked at the three fires burning in the garden: The Red Fire of Mars, the Golden Light of Mercury, and the Smoky Flame of Rahu.

Aruna: "Venus is brave, Surya. With Mars, she risks burning in the fire of passion. With Mercury, she risks fading into superficiality. With Rahu, she risks getting lost in the smoke of illusion."

Surya: "Desire is the greatest risk of all, Charioteer. But without it, the world would be gray. We have seen how the Planets mix in the open field. But now, we must look at the **Geography of the Battle**. What happens when these mixtures occur in specific Houses? What happens when the Sun and Moon meet in the 10th House versus the 4th House? This is the **Master Key**. This is the concept of **Takkar** (Collision). Prepare yourself. We are about to learn how to read the map of war. Turn the page to **Chapter 15**."

CHAPTER 15: CONJUNCTIONS IN SPECIFIC HOUSES

(The Master Key: The Geography of the Battle)

The Map Of War

The Chariot halted at the edge of a great, vertigo-inducing precipice. Below them, the landscape of the Zodiac stretched out not as a list of abstract concepts, but as a sprawling, physical kingdom. From this divine height, Aruna could see the entire board at once. It was a terrifying and magnificent geometry.

To the East lay the Red Fortress of the 1st House, its walls bristling with the spears of Mars. To the North lay the Blue Ocean of the 4th House, calm and infinite. To the South, the Black Mines of the 10th House belched smoke and dust, the sound of hammers ringing against iron. And to the West, the Golden Temple of the 9th House shone like a beacon on a hill.

Aruna wiped the sweat from his brow. The journey through the alchemical mixtures of Part IV had been exhausting. He had seen Fire mix with Water to create the steam of ambition. He had seen Light mix with Smoke to create the illusion of glamour. He had seen the Moon poisoned by Saturn and agitated by Mercury.

Aruna: "O Surya, we have learned the chemistry. We know that Moon + Sun creates Marble, and Moon + Saturn creates Poison. We know the formulas. But looking at this map below... I have a question. Does the *container* matter? If I pour the Poison of Moon + Saturn into a lead cup, it stays poison. But what if I pour it into a golden chalice? Does the 'Harvest' of the Sun-Moon conjunction grow the same way in the dry Desert of the 5th House as it does in the fertile River of the 4th? Is the chemistry absolute, or is it relative?"

Surya: "You have asked the question that separates the novice from the Master, Aruna. Chemistry is universal, but Geography is specific. A fire in a fireplace warms the house and cooks the food. The same fire, with the same intensity, burning in a library destroys history. We have studied the **Mixtures** (*Yuti*). Now we must study the **Placement** (*Sthana*). This is the **Master Key** of the *Lal Kitab*. The same combination can be a blessing in one house and a curse in another. This is the concept of **Takkar** (Collision). We must learn to read the map of war. We must learn why the Sun and Moon are Kings in the 4th, but Blind Beggars in the 10th. We must learn why Venus and Mars are creative lovers in the 3rd, but murderers in the 7th. Prepare yourself. We are about to descend into the specific battlefields. We are going to see how the ground beneath your feet changes the fight."

The Takkar Concept: The Physics Of Collision

The Law of the Landlord In the *Lal Kitab*, planets do not float in empty space. They inhabit "Houses" (*Ghar*). Every House has a **Permanent Resident** (*Pukka Ghar Owner*) and a **Significator** (*Karaka*). These are the Landlords. When a Conjunction (two planets) enters a house, they are guests entering someone else's home. The outcome of the visit depends entirely on whether the Landlord likes the Guests.

- **The Metaphor of the Guest:** Imagine **Sun + Moon** as a **Royal Couple** (The King and Queen).
  - If the Royal Couple visits a **Temple** (9th House/Jupiter), the Priest (Jupiter) welcomes them. He gives them the best seat. The King bows to the God. The Queen feels safe. The result is **"Pious Wealth."** The environment supports their nature.
  - But if the Royal Couple walks into a **Coal Mine** (10th House/Saturn), the situation changes. The mine is dirty. It is dark. The miners (Saturn) do not care about royalty; they care about coal. The King's robes get stained. The Queen feels cold and frightened. The King tries to give orders, but his voice is drowned out by the machinery.
  - The combination (Sun + Moon) is the same.

The people are the same. But the result changes from 'Wealth' to 'Blindness' purely based on the location.

The Dialogue: The Guest and the Host

Aruna: "So it is not enough to know the guests; we must know the host?"

Surya: "Precisely. In every analysis, you must ask three questions:

1. **Who are the Guests?** (The Conjunction, e.g., Venus + Mars).
2. **Who is the Landlord?** (The Ruler of the House, e.g., Saturn in the 10th).
3. **What is the relationship?** (Does the Landlord hate the Guest?) If the Landlord hates the Guest, the Guest will be 'poisoned' by the house. This is the **Takkar**. When the energy of the *Planets* collides with the energy of the *House*, a third reality is born."

Case Study 1: The Royal Couple (Sun + Moon)

(The Difference between Day and Night)

Let us look at the most powerful combination: The Parents. The Soul (Sun) and the Mind (Moon).

Scenario A: Sun + Moon in House 4 *(The King and Queen in the Water Palace)*

- **The Chemistry:**
  - Sun (**Fire/King**) + Moon (**Water/Queen**) = Amavasya (New Moon).
  - Astronomically, this is dark.
- **The Geography:**
  - **House 4** is the Moon's Pukka Ghar (Permanent Home). It is the River.
- **The Takkar (Collision):**

- Here, the Moon is in her own castle. She is strong. She is the Hostess.
- The Sun (Guest) is a friend of the Moon.
- The Fire of the Sun warms the Water of the 4th. It creates a "Warm Bath." It is not a forest fire; it is a heated pool.

- **The Result: The Full Moon Effect.**
  - Even though it is astronomically a New Moon (Dark), the *Lal Kitab* says this placement acts like a **Full Moon** (*Purnima*).
  - **The Native:** He is incredibly wealthy. His mother is powerful and lives long. His peace of mind is absolute. He has the authority of the King but the softness of the Mother.
  - *Why?* Because the "River" (4th) washes away the darkness of the Amavasya. The environment (Water) supports the Moon so strongly that she cannot be burnt by the Sun.

Scenario B: Sun + Moon in House 10 *(The King and Queen in the Coal Mine)*

- **The Chemistry:**
  - Sun + Moon = The Parents.
- **The Geography:**
  - **House 10** is Saturn's Home (Darkness/Iron/Cold).
- **The Takkar (Collision):**
  - Saturn hates the Sun. (Darkness hates Light).
  - Saturn freezes the Moon. (Ice blocks Water).
  - The 10th House is "Noon" (Sun's peak position), but it is also the "Grave of Comfort."
  - Here, the Landlord (Saturn) attacks both guests.
- **The Result: The Blind Planets.**
  - Here, the "Water" (Moon) freezes into "Black Ice."
  - The "Fire" (Sun) is suffocated by coal dust.
  - **The Native:** He suffers from **Suspicion**. He doubts his own parents. He doubts his wife. He feels the world is

against him.
    - **Physical Symptom:** He may have weak eyesight or go blind (Sun/Moon govern eyes).
    - **The Conflict:** The Sun tries to rule (Career), but Saturn blocks him with delays. The Moon tries to feel, but Saturn numbs her with cynicism. The native becomes a "Cruel Administrator"—efficient, but dead inside.

The Remedial Logic:

- **In House 4:** Do nothing. Enjoy the blessing. Do not disturb the water.
- **In House 10:** You cannot fight Saturn in his own house. You cannot make the Sun "hotter" to melt the ice (that would cause an explosion). You must use **Mars** (Friend of Sun/ Moon and Enemy of Saturn).
    - *Remedy:* Wear a **Copper Coin** (Sun) around the neck (Ascendant). This lifts the Sun out of the "Mine" (10th) and places it in the "Head" (1st). It separates the King from the Coal.

Case Study 2: The Lover (Venus + Mars)

(The Difference between Art and War)

Let us look at the combination of Passion: Venus (Beauty) and Mars (Force).

Scenario A: Venus + Mars in House 3 *(The Artist in the Studio)*

- **The Chemistry:**
    - Venus (**Beauty**) + Mars (**Energy**) = Passion/Creativity.
- **The Geography:**
    - **House 3** belongs to **Mercury** (Communication) and **Mars** (Courage).
- **The Takkar (Collision):**
    - Mars is the co-landlord here. He is comfortable. He has his weapons.

    - Venus is the guest. Mars (Landlord) protects Venus (Lover).
    - Mercury (House 3) gives "Voice" and "Skill" to the creation.
- **The Result: The Genius Artist.**
    - The "Fire" is channeled into skill. The native becomes a great writer, painter, actor, or surgeon.
    - The passion is expressed through *work*, not conflict. The native seduces the world through his art. The "War" is fought on canvas or paper.

Scenario B: Venus + Mars in House 7 *(The Lovers in the Battlefield)*

- **The Chemistry:**
    - Venus + Mars = Passion/Sex.
- **The Geography:**
    - **House 7** is Venus's Home (Marriage).
- **The Takkar (Collision):**
    - Venus is at home. She wants peace, partnership, and harmony.
    - Mars is the **Invader** here. In the 7th House, Mars is *Ku-Mangal* (Bad Mars). He brings a Sword into the Bedroom.
    - The Landlord (Venus) is overpowered by the Guest (Mars).
- **The Result: The Burning Marriage.**
    - The passion turns into jealousy, possessiveness, and violence.
    - The native beats his wife (Mars attacking Venus) or suffers from blood disorders.
    - The "Fire" burns the "Silk" of the relationship. The bed catches fire.
    - This is the placement of **"Manglik Dosha"** in its most aggressive form.

The Remedial Logic:

- **In House 3:** Encourage the native to write, play sports, or debate. Channel the energy outward.
- **In House 7:** You must cool the Mars. You cannot remove him, but you can sedate him.
    - *Remedy:* Keep a **Solid Silver Ball** (Moon) in the pocket.
    - *The Physics:* Silver is Moon. Moon is the Mother. When the Mother enters the room, the angry Warrior (Mars) calms down. The Silver Ball acts as a "Coolant" for the 7th House heat.
    - *Remedy:* Bury an earthen pot (*Budh*) filled with Honey (*Mars*). This "grounds" the Mars energy into the earth, preventing it from burning the Venus air.

Case Study 3: The Eclipse (Moon + Ketu)

(The Difference between Mysticism and Poverty)

Let us look at the combination of the Mind (Moon) and the Void (Ketu).

Scenario A: Moon + Ketu in House 12 *(The Monk in the Monastery)*

- **The Chemistry:**
    - Moon (**Mind**) + Ketu (**Detachment**) = Void/Silence.
- **The Geography:**
    - **House 12** is the natural place for "Letting Go," Sleep, and Moksha.
    - Ketu is the *Moksha Karaka*. He is happy here. He owns the "Flag" on the roof.
    - The 12th House is the Ocean.
- **The Takkar (Collision):**
    - The Moon dissolves into the "Ocean of God."
    - The "Eclipse" blocks the *World*, not the *Spirit*.
- **The Result: The Enlightened Saint.**
    - The native sleeps peacefully. His dreams are pro-

phetic. He is detached from material worries because he understands the illusion. He does not hold onto pain. The Vacuum becomes a space for God to enter.

Scenario B: Moon + Ketu in House 6 *(The Patient in the Asylum)*

- **The Chemistry:**
  - Moon + Ketu = Void/Fear.
- **The Geography:**
  - **House 6** is **Mercury** (Nerves) + **Ketu** (Underworld).
  - It is the "Deep Well."
- **The Takkar (Collision):**
  - Mercury (Landlord) hates the Moon.
  - Ketu (Co-Landlord) is the "Biting Dog" here.
  - The Moon is trapped in a deep well with a dog and a critic. There is no escape.
- **The Result: The Paralyzed Mind.**
  - The "Detachment" turns into "Dissociation." The native loses touch with reality.
  - The "Void" becomes "Depression."
  - The native's mother suffers from mysterious pains (Ketu) that doctors cannot diagnose.
  - The Takkar here sucks the "Life Force" of the Moon into the disease sector.

The Remedial Logic:

- **In House 12:** Meditate. The combination is spiritual. No remedy is needed unless insomnia is present.
- **In House 6:** You must separate the Dog (Ketu) from the Water (Moon).
  - *Remedy:* Wear **Gold** in the ears.
  - *The Physics:* Gold is Jupiter. The Ear is Ketu's organ. Jupiter controls Ketu. The Guru tames the Dog.
  - *Remedy:* Feed dogs (Ketu) far away from the house. Do not let the dog enter the bedroom.

The Remedial Strategy: Identifying The Attacker

Aruna: "The map is complex, Surya. In a war between two planets in a specific house, how do I know which one to save and which one to suppress? Do I save the Moon, or do I fight Saturn? Do I feed the Tiger, or do I hide the Lamb?"

Surya: "There is a **Golden Rule** in the *Lal Kitab*, Aruna. Write this in the center of your ledger: **Remedy the Attacker, Protect the Victim.** In a conjunction, one planet is usually the **Aggressor** (The one causing harm) and the other is the **Victim** (The one suffering).

- **Moon + Saturn:**
  - *The Dynamic:* Saturn (Poison) attacks Moon (Milk). The Moon does not attack Saturn.
  - *Strategy:* We do not strengthen the Moon (adding more Milk just wastes it). We **tame Saturn**.
  - *The Action:* We feed the snakes (Saturn) or bury the oil (Saturn). We neutralize the poison.
- **Venus + Rahu:**
  - *The Dynamic:* Rahu (Smoke) clouds Venus (Mirror). Venus does not hurt Rahu.
  - *Strategy:* We do not polish the Mirror (Venus). We **clear the Smoke** (Rahu).
  - *The Action:* We bury the Blue Flower (Rahu) or keep Lead (Rahu) in the pocket. We ground the demon.
- **Sun + Venus:**
  - *The Dynamic:* Sun (Heat) burns Venus (Flower).
  - *Strategy:* We do not water the flower (it will boil). We **shade the Sun**.
  - *The Action:* We use Copper coins (Sun) thrown in water, or heavy Earth (Saturn) to block the heat. We ask the King to step back.

The Master Key is Diagnosis. You must look at the House. If the

Landlord of the House is friends with the Aggressor, the battle is bloody (e.g., Sun+Moon in 10th - Saturn helps the darkness). If the Landlord is friends with the Victim, there is hope for a treaty (e.g., Sun+Moon in 4th - Moon helps the light).

You are the Diplomat of the Stars, Aruna. You must negotiate the peace treaty using the elements of nature."

Summary Of Part Iv

Aruna rolled up the great map of the Zodiac. The landscape seemed less chaotic now. He understood that the planets were not random wanderers, but actors on a stage, constrained by the set design of the Houses.

Aruna: "We have learned the Chemistry of Association (Chapter 12-14). We have learned the Geography of the Battle (Chapter 15). We know *what* happens when planets mix, and *where* it happens. The diagnosis is complete."

Surya: "The diagnosis of the *Present* is complete, Charioteer. But the Chariot does not just travel in the Present. It carries a heavy trunk in the back. That trunk is full of **Old Debts**. The sins of the Grandfather block the path of the Grandson. The tears of the Mother become the poverty of the Son. We must now open the **Ancestral Ledger**. We must learn about **Pitra Rin** (Father's Debt), **Matru Rin** (Mother's Debt), and **Stri Rin** (Wife's Debt). We must learn why a man born innocent might suffer for a crime committed a hundred years ago. Prepare yourself, Aruna. We are about to enter the haunted archives of the bloodline. We enter **Part V: The Ancestral Ledger**. Turn the page to **Chapter 16**."

PART V: THE ANCESTRAL LEDGER

(Decoding the Rinas: Debts of the Bloodline)

CHAPTER 16: THE MOTHER'S DEBT (MATRU RIN)

(The Blocked River: Ketu in the 4th House)

The Opening Of The Vault

The Chariot came to a shuddering halt. The noise of the battlefields, the haggling of the marketplaces, and the soft whispers of the gardens faded into a heavy, suffocating silence. The air grew still, as if the wind itself was afraid to move.

Aruna and Surya stood before a massive, iron-bound door set into the side of a sheer granite mountain. The door was ancient, covered in layers of rust, moss, and the dust of centuries. It had no handle. It had no keyhole. It was sealed not by a lock, but by the weight of time itself.

Aruna felt a chill that had nothing to do with the temperature. It was a cold that seeped into his bones—the chill of history, of secrets long buried but never dead.

Aruna: "O Surya, we have traveled through the twelve houses. We have seen the Moon fight Saturn in the dark and Venus embrace Mars in the fire. We have diagnosed the present condition of the Chariot. We have fixed the wheels and oiled the axles. Why do we stop here? What lies behind this door that feels so heavy?"

Surya: "Behind this door lies the **Past**, Aruna. Until now, we have looked at the horoscope as a map of the individual's life. We assumed that the native starts with a clean slate—a fresh sheet of paper upon which he writes his destiny. But that is a lie. No man is born alone. He is born as a link in a chain. He carries the genetic code of his ancestors in his blood, and he carries their karmic code in his soul. This is **Part V: The Ancestral Ledger**. The Chariot does not just carry the Passenger; it carries a heavy trunk in the back, bolted to the frame. That trunk is full of **Rinas** (Debts). The sins of the Grandfather block the path of the Grandson. The tears of the Mother become the poverty of the Son. The curse of the Wife becomes the illness of the Husband. We must now learn to read the **Ledger of Debts**. We must learn why a man born innocent might suffer for a crime committed a hundred years ago. We must learn how to pay the bill that was left unpaid by those who came before us. And we begin with the most primal debt of all: **Matru Rin**—The Debt of the Mother."

The Anatomy Of Matru Rin

(The Eclipse in the Heart)

The Architecture of the Blockage In the *Lal Kitab*, specific planetary placements act as "Flags" indicating that the native has inherited a karmic debt related to a specific ancestor. These are not random afflictions; they are specific signals. **Matru Rin** (Mother's Debt) is signaled by a very precise and dangerous combination: **Ketu in the 4th House**.

Let us analyze the chemistry of this collision:

- **The 4th House:** This is the domain of the **Moon**. It represents the **River**, the **Heart**, the **Home**, the **Peace of Mind**, and the **Mother**. It is the source of all nourishment. It is the "Milk" of life.
- **Ketu:** This is the **Dragon's Tail**. It represents **Cutting**, **Blocking**, **Detachment**, **Mistakes**, and the **Termite**. It is the energy of separation.

When Ketu sits in the 4th House, it is an invasion. The Dragon's Tail is thrashing in the Mother's River. It acts like a **Dam** made of rubble and thorns. It blocks the flow of water. It turns the "River of Plenty" into a "Dry Bed." This placement indicates that in a past generation, the Mother (or a mother-figure/ancestor) was deeply wronged, neglected, or suffered immensely. That trauma was not resolved; it was buried. And like a buried landmine, it has waited for this generation to explode.

The Dialogue: The Termite in the Foundation

Aruna: "I see a beautiful house sitting by the riverbank, Surya. It looks perfect from the outside. But when I look closer, I see that the walls are hollow. Termites are eating the wood from the inside out. The river outside is dry, just a bed of cracked mud and stones. What happened here?"

Surya: "The Ancestors neglected the **Source**, Aruna. Perhaps a grandmother was thrown out of the house by her in-laws. Perhaps a mother died in childbirth, unmourned and unremembered, her sacrifice taken for granted. Perhaps the family grew rich by selling milk (Mother's essence) unethically, mixing it with water or blood. Whatever the specific cause, the result is **Matru Rin**. Ketu in the 4th House acts like a parasite. It eats the peace. The native works hard, but his 'Liquid Cash' evaporates. Money comes in one hand and leaves from the other. He seeks peace, but his mind is always anxious, vibrating with an unknown fear. He tries to build a home, but the walls crack, the pipes leak, and the family fights. He is paying the interest on a loan he never signed. He is carrying the grief of a woman he may never have met."

The Symptoms of the Debt

How do we confirm if the native is suffering from Matru Rin? The *Lal Kitab* gives specific diagnostic markers—physical and environmental signs that manifest in the life of the native.

1. **The Drying of Liquid Cash:** The native may have assets (property/gold/land), but he has no *cash*. He is "Asset Rich, Cash Poor." When he needs 100 rupees, he cannot find it. Money comes in and immediately goes out on illness, repairs, or waste. The river doesn't flow; it stagnates or drains away.
2. **The Illness of the Mother:** The native's mother is often sickly, emotionally distant, or suffers from a difficult life. Or, the native is separated from her early (boarding school/adoption). The relationship is strained or tragic.
3. **The Animal Sign:** The native may have a dog (Ketu)

that dies suddenly, runs away, or becomes aggressive. Or, if the family owns a cow (Venus/Moon), it stops giving milk or dies. The animals sense the Ketu energy.

4. **The Mental State:** Depression, lack of mental peace, and a pervasive feeling of being "unloved" even when surrounded by family. The Heart (4th House) feels empty, like a room with no furniture.

The Parable Of The Dried Well

- **The Passenger:** A man named Dev. He is a hard worker, honest, skilled, and devout. He comes from what everyone calls a "good family." He does everything right.
- **The Struggle:** Despite his efforts, Dev cannot save money. It is a mathematical impossibility in his life. Every time his savings account hits 10,000 rupees, a disaster strikes—his mother falls ill, his car engine explodes, or a pipe bursts in his house—costing exactly 10,000 rupees. He feels like he is running on a treadmill, sweating but moving nowhere.
- **The House:** He lives in an ancestral home. The house feels heavy. It is always dusty, no matter how much they clean. The taps leak constantly, defying the plumber. There is a sense of sorrow in the walls.
- **The Investigation:** Dev visits a *Lal Kitab* astrologer. The astrologer looks at his chart and points to a single placement: **Ketu in the 4th House.**
    - The Astrologer asks: "Did your grandfather mistreat his wife? Or did someone in the family throw a widow out of the house? Or did you neglect a cow?"
    - Dev investigates the family history. He speaks to an old aunt. He finds out that his great-grandmother was indeed treated cruelly after her husband died. She was denied food, locked in a room, and eventually turned out of the house. She cursed the lineage as she left.
- **The Diagnosis:** The family is suffering from **Matru Rin**.

The tears of the great-grandmother have become the poverty of the great-grandson. The Moon (Mother) is blocked by Ketu (The Curse). The River has been dammed by the sin of the ancestors.

The Remedial Logic: The Silver Coins

To clear Matru Rin, we cannot just pray. Prayer is for the soul; this is a debt of the blood. We must perform a physical, alchemical act of **Restitution**. We must unblock the river using the metal of the Moon.

The Great Remedy: The Silver Flow

- **The Prescription:** Collect **Silver Coins** (or square pieces of silver) from *every blood relative* (Grandfather, Father, Uncles, Brothers). Everyone must contribute an equal amount (e.g., one coin each or equal value).
    1. *Note:* Sisters and daughters are not included in this specific bloodline remedy (as they go to another lineage/gotra after marriage), but the male lineage must contribute.
- **The Ritual:** On the same day, take all these collected coins and throw them together into a **Flowing River**.
- **The Alchemical Physics:**
    1. **Silver** is the metal of the **Moon**. It represents the Mother's essence, peace, purity, and forgiveness.
    2. **The River** is the **4th House** in motion. It is the cosmic bloodstream. It is the only force capable of washing away the stagnation of Ketu.
    3. **The Joint Contribution:** The debt is "Ancestral," meaning it belongs to the whole bloodline, not just the native. By collecting silver from everyone, you are acknowledging the *collective* responsibility. You are pooling the family's "Moon Energy." You are saying, "We are all in this together."

4. **The Act:** Throwing the silver into the river is an act of **Returning the Moon to the Moon**. You are offering the "Price of the Mother" back to the Universal Mother. You are saying, "We return what was taken. We offer silver to heal the waters. We pay the debt."
5. **The Result:** The silver sinks. It creates a "foundation" in the riverbed. The blockage of Ketu is washed away by the heavy influx of pure Moon energy. The curse is lifted. The river begins to flow again. The "Liquid Cash" returns.

Secondary Remedies (If Joint Family is Impossible)

Sometimes, the family is estranged, and a joint ritual is impossible. In that case, the native must act alone, but with greater intensity.

1. **Milk for the Dogs:**
   - *The Prescription:* Feed **Milk** to **Stray Dogs**.
   - *The Physics:*
     - Dogs represent **Ketu**.
     - Milk represents **Moon**.
     - Usually, Moon and Ketu are enemies. But by *feeding* the dog, you turn the enemy into a dependent. You satisfy Ketu's hunger with the Moon's abundance. You tell the "Termite" to eat the food, not the foundation. You make peace with the Dragon.
2. **The Yellow Lemon:**
   - *The Prescription:* Float **Yellow Lemons** in the river.
   - *The Physics:*
     - Yellow is **Jupiter**.
     - Jupiter is the only planet that can control Ketu (The Guru tames the Disciple).
     - By sending Jupiter (Lemon) into the Moon's house (River), you bring the "Guru" to mediate the conflict. You ask for divine intervention to clear

the blockage.

The Warning Of The False Mother

Aruna: "Is it truly that simple, Surya? Can a few silver coins wash away the sins of a century? Can metal cure a broken heart?"

Surya: "The coins are the *Token*, Aruna. The *Intent* is the currency. But there is a danger—a trap that many fall into. If the native performs the remedy but continues to disrespect his **Living Mother**, the remedy will backfire. The Living Mother is the visible manifestation of the Moon God. If he throws silver in the river but shouts at his mother at home, he is a hypocrite. He is adding fresh insult to the old injury. The Ketu in the 4th House will see this hypocrisy. It will turn into a rabid dog and bite him harder. The debt will double. The remedy clears the *Past* debt. The native's behavior determines the *Present* credit. He must become the **Servant of the Mother**. He must touch her feet. He must never argue with her, even if she is wrong. He must treat her as the deity of the temple. Because for him, she is not just a woman; she is the **Deity of his Luck**. If she cries, his bank account bleeds."

Summary Of The Mother's Debt

Aruna looked at the closed door of the mountain. He understood now that the door was not locked by a key, but by a tear. And it could only be opened by a tear of repentance.

Aruna: "Matru Rin is the blockage of Love, Surya. It is the dried riverbed where nothing grows. It is the hunger that food cannot fill."

Surya: "Correct. And until the River flows, the Garden of Venus cannot bloom. You cannot have a happy Wife (Venus) if you have an angry Mother (Moon). The structure collapses. We have cleared the first debt. But there are other debts in the trunk. There is the debt of the **Wife** (*Stri Rin*)—when Venus is cursed. There is the debt of the **Unborn Child** (*Santan Rin*). There is the debt of the **Cruelty to Nature** (*Kudrati Rin*). The Ancestral Ledger is thick, Charioteer. It is filled with red ink. We must now turn to the next page. We must look at what happens when the **Sun** (The King) himself acts against the **Venus** (The Wife). Turn the page to **Chapter 17**."

CHAPTER 17: THE WIFE'S DEBT (STRI RIN)

(The Cursed Hearth: Sun, Moon, and Rahu Afflicting Venus)

The Second Vault

The heavy iron door of the Mountain of Debts groaned in protest as Aruna pushed it further open. They had just cleared the first chamber—the dark, damp, subterranean room of the Mother's Debt (*Matru Rin*). The air there had smelled of stagnant water, wet clay, and old grief. It was the smell of a river that had stopped flowing.

But as they stepped deeper into the mountain, crossing the threshold into the Second Vault, the atmosphere changed violently.

The second chamber was not damp. It was hot. The air was dry and scorched, as if a great fire had raged here long ago and only recently died down. The walls were blackened with soot. The floor was covered in gray ash that swirled around their feet.

In the center of the room stood a statue of a breathtakingly beautiful woman, carved from white marble. But the statue was damaged. Her face was cracked down the middle. Her hands were bound with chains made of black smoke. At her feet lay a broken mirror and a withered rose.

Aruna felt a sudden, sharp pain in his chest—not physical pain, but the acute ache of a heart that has been broken a thousand times. He felt a wave of loneliness so profound it made him gasp.

Aruna: "O Surya, the air here burns. It tastes of anger, betrayal, and unshed tears. The Mother's Debt was sad, a quiet tragedy. But this... this feels violent. It feels like a crime scene. What happened here? Who is this woman bound in smoke? Why is her beauty scarred?"

Surya: "This is the **Chamber of the Wife**, Aruna. We have entered the domain of **Stri Rin** (The Wife's Debt). The Mother gives life, but the Wife sustains it. She is the **Lakshmi** of the house. She is the keeper of the hearth, the dignity of the family, and the vessel of Venus. She is the 'Shakti' that allows the 'Shiva' to act. But in this lineage, a crime was committed against her. Perhaps a wife was beaten into silence by a tyrannical husband. Perhaps she was cast out on the street for another woman. Perhaps she was murdered for her dowry, or driven to suicide by cruelty. Or perhaps, in a previous generation, a man used the 'Fire' of his Authority (Sun) or the 'Smoke' of his Deceit (Rahu) to destroy the 'Flower' of his life (Venus). The result is a curse that burns through the bloodline like a slow fever. The men of this family cannot hold onto happiness. They marry, but the marriage turns to ash. They earn gold, but the wealth (Lakshmi) vanishes before they can count it. We must now learn how to heal the burned flower. We must learn how to pay the debt of the Goddess."

The Anatomy Of Stri Rin

(The War on Venus)

The Architecture of the Curse In the *Lal Kitab*, **Stri Rin** is not a vague moral concept. It is a specific planetary configuration that signals a history of systematic abuse against the feminine principle (Venus). The debt is activated when the **Enemies of Venus** attack her in specific houses, turning the "Planet of Love" into the "Planet of Vengeance."

The Primary Culprits:

1. **The Sun (The Tyrant King):**
   - *The Dynamic:* When the Sun sits in the **5th**, **7th**, or **9th House** and is afflicted or attacks Venus.

- *The Crime:* This represents the **Ego of the Husband** destroying the Wife. It is the King who treats his Queen as a slave. It is authority used to crush, not protect.

2. **The Moon (The Jealous Mother):**
   - *The Dynamic:* When the Moon is weak, Kemadruma (lonely), or sits with malefic planets like Ketu, and attacks Venus.
   - *The Crime:* This represents the **Mother-in-Law** destroying the Daughter-in-Law. It is the "Milk" poisoning the "Curd." It is the failure of the feminine to protect the feminine.
3. **Rahu (The Deceiver):**
   - *The Dynamic:* This is the most common and dangerous cause. When Rahu attacks Venus (or sits in Venus's houses 2 or 7).
   - *The Crime:* This represents **Deceit**, **Adultery**, and **Objectification**. It signifies an ancestor who kept mistresses, cheated his wife, or treated women as disposable objects of pleasure. It is the "Smoke" choking the "Breath."

The Diagnostic Signature: How do you know if a chart carries the heavy load of **Stri Rin**? The *Lal Kitab* gives a precise formula: **"If Venus, Moon, or Rahu are in the 2nd, 7th, or 12th houses and are afflicted, the debt exists."** But the most potent sign is not in the chart; it is in the life of the native.

The Symptoms of the Debt:

1. **Marital Chaos:** The native struggles to get married. Obstacles arise constantly. If he does marry, the wife is chronically ill, hostile, or emotionally distant. The home becomes a battlefield.
2. **The Celebration Curse:** Every time there is a "Happy Occasion" (*Shubh Karya*) in the family—a wedding, a birth, a festival—a fight breaks out, or a tragedy occurs.

The "Joy" (Venus) is cursed. The laughter turns to screaming.

3. **The Vanishing Wealth:** The native earns well. He is capable. But the moment he brings the money home, it disappears on "Useless Things" (*Fizool Kharch*), illnesses, or theft. Lakshmi refuses to stay in a house where she was once insulted.
4. **The Skin and Blood:** The native or his wife suffers from skin diseases (Venus rules skin), hormonal imbalances, or blood disorders. The body rejects its own beauty.

The Dialogue: The Statue's Tears

Aruna: "I see the logic, O Light. If the Ancestors treated the Wife as a slave or a victim, the energy of Venus in the bloodline became twisted. It became a 'Negative Venus.' Instead of bringing love, she brings vengeance."

Surya: "Precisely. Energy cannot be destroyed; it can only be transformed. The tears of the grandmother become the divorce of the grandson. The bruises of the wife become the poverty of the husband. The Universe keeps a strict ledger. You cannot harm the 'Goddess of Wealth' (Wife) and expect to keep the 'Wealth' (Money). They are the same frequency. You cannot kick the idol and expect the blessing."

The Parable Of The Golden Cage

- **The Passenger:** A man named Rajan. He is handsome, wealthy, and successful in business. He drives luxury cars and lives in a mansion. To the outside world, he has everything.
- **The Curse:** But inside his home, there is only death and silence.
  - His **first wife** died mysteriously within a year of marriage.
  - His **second wife** ran away with his driver, taking his

jewelry.

  - His **third wife** is chronically depressed, locks herself in her room, and refuses to speak to him.

- **The Pattern:** Rajan is not a "bad" man in the conventional sense. But he is **Arrogant** (Sun). He believes his money buys him the right to control. He interrupts his wife. He dismisses her feelings. He treats his wives like trophies (Rahu) to be displayed, not souls to be loved.
- **The Ancestral History:** The Astrologer looks at his chart and sees **Sun and Rahu in the 7th House** (The House of Marriage). This is a "Solar Eclipse" in the bedroom.
  - **The Inquiry:** "Did your grandfather have a mistress? Did he throw his first wife out of the house? Or did he lock her up?"
  - **The Truth:** Rajan goes pale. He admits that his grandfather was a powerful feudal landlord who kept many women. He beat his legitimate wife regularly and eventually locked her in a room—a "Golden Cage"—where she died of grief and starvation, cursing his name.
- **The Diagnosis:** This is **Stri Rin**. The grandfather's cruelty has become the grandson's loneliness. The "Golden Cage" has become a "Golden Prison" for Rajan himself. He cannot keep a wife because his lineage has declared war on the Wife archetype.

The Remedial Logic: The 100 Cows

To clear Stri Rin, we cannot use a small remedy. We cannot just light a lamp. The offense was against the **Life Force** (Venus/ Shakti). The repayment must be massive. It must be biological. We must invoke the supreme earthly form of Venus: **The Cow** (*Gau Mata*).

The Great Remedy: Feeding 100 Cows

- **The Prescription:** The native must feed **100 Cows** in a single day.
    1. *The Variation:* If feeding 100 cows in one day is impossible, he can feed **100 portions** of fodder to cows over a period of time, or get the blessing of 100 separate cows. But the "Single Day" ritual is the most potent for breaking the chain.
- **The Ritual:** The native must go to a *Gaushala* (Cow Shelter). He must buy high-quality **Green Fodder** (*Chara*)—green represents Mercury, the friend of Venus. He must feed the cows with his own hands. He must touch the cows, apologize to them in his heart, and ask for the release of the debt.
- **The Alchemical Physics:**
    1. **The Cow is Venus:** In Vedic alchemy, the Cow is the "Living Temple" of Venus. She represents the Earthly Mother, the Nurturer, and the ultimate form of passive, giving love. She gives milk (Moon) and eats grass (Mercury), harmonizing the domestic energies.
    2. **The Number 100:** This is not a random number. It represents "Completeness" or "Cent." It signifies a *massive* repayment. It overwhelms the negative karma with a flood of positive merit. It is an avalanche of grace.
    3. **The Sun-Venus Harmonization:** Cows (Venus) need the Sun to produce milk. By feeding them, the native (acting as the Sun/Provider) serves Venus. He reverses the ancestral dynamic. Instead of the "King beating the Wife," the "King serves the Wife." He bows before the feminine.
    4. **The Result:** The blessings of 100 cows create a "White Shield" around the native's Venus. The "Burnt Flower" begins to heal. The wife's health improves. The wealth stabilizes. The curse is lifted by the breath of the cows.

Secondary Remedies (The Daily Maintenance)

While the 100 Cows ritual breaks the lock, the native must perform daily maintenance to keep the door open. He must change his behavior.

1. **The Coin from the In-Laws:**
    - *The Prescription:* The native should take a **Silver Coin** from his in-laws (Wife's family) and keep it in his safe/ locker forever.
    - *The Alchemical Physics:*
        - **Silver** is **Moon.**
        - The **In-laws** represent the **House of Venus** (7th House/Venus domain).
        - By humbly asking for and accepting a silver coin, the native is bowing to the "Wife's Lineage." He is accepting the "Blessing of the Feminine." It heals the rift between the two families. It anchors the "Lakshmi" in the house.
2. **Donating Clothes:**
    - *The Prescription:* Donate beautiful, new clothes to poor women or widows.
    - *The Physics:* Clothes represent **Venus** (appearance/ dignity). Giving dignity (clothes) to women who have none reverses the ancestral karma of "stripping dignity" from the wife.
3. **The Smile of the Wife:**
    - *The Law:* The native must ensure his wife never sleeps crying.
    - *The Logic:* The tears of the wife are the "acid" that dissolves the husband's luck. Her smile is the "alkali" that neutralizes the debt. This is not just morality; it is survival mechanics. If the wife is unhappy, the 7th House (Daily Income) collapses.

The Alchemy Of The Three Enemies

(Decoding the Sun, Moon, and Rahu Attacks)

Aruna: "But Surya, you said the debt comes from the Sun, Moon, or Rahu. Does the remedy change depending on who the attacker is? Is the cure for a Burn different from the cure for a Poison?"

Surya: "You are sharp, Charioteer. Yes, the *flavor* of the remedy shifts slightly."

Case A: The Sun Attack (Ego-Based Debt)

- *The Crime:* The ancestor used authority to crush the wife. He was a tyrant.
- *The Specific Remedy:* The native must **bow** to his wife. He must give her **Gold** (Sun's metal) to wear. This puts the "Sun" on the "Venus," but as an ornament, not a shackle. He must let her lead in family matters.

Case B: The Moon Attack (Mother-Based Debt)

- *The Crime:* The ancestor allowed his mother to abuse his wife. The "Milk" poisoned the "Curd."
- *The Specific Remedy:* The native must make peace between his mother and wife. He must weigh his wife against **Rice/ Milk** and donate it (Tula Daan). This pays off the Moon's jealousy.

Case C: The Rahu Attack (Deceit-Based Debt)

- *The Crime:* The ancestor had secret affairs, cheated the wife, or treated her as a sex object.
- *The Specific Remedy:* The native must **never** lie to his wife. He must bury a **Blue Flower** (Rahu) in the earth (Venus) to "ground" the deceit. And he must feed the 100 Cows specifically with **Green Grass** (Mercury) to bring intelligence back to the relationship.

The Warning Of The Relapsed King

Aruna stood before the statue of the bound woman. The smoke around her hands seemed to be thinning, but her eyes were still sad.

Aruna: "Will the debt return, Surya? If the native feeds the cows today, is he free forever? Can he go back to his old ways?"

Surya: "The debt is cleared, but the *tendency* remains, Aruna. The native carries the genetic code of the Tyrant. The anger is in his blood. If he relapses—if he raises his hand against his wife, or if he cheats on her—the debt returns with **Compound Interest**. The *Lal Kitab* is unforgiving here. For a man with Stri Rin, his wife is his **Talisman**. If she leaves him, his luck leaves him. If she dies, his empire crumbles. He must treat her not just as a partner, but as the **Keeper of his Soul**. He must serve her to save himself. He must become the Charioteer who serves the Passenger."

Summary Of The Wife's Debt

Aruna bowed to the statue. He placed a small white flower at her feet. The heat in the room seemed to dissipate, replaced by a cool breeze carrying the scent of jasmine.

Aruna: "Stri Rin is the blockage of Joy, Surya. Matru Rin blocked the Peace (Water). Stri Rin blocks the Pleasure (Fire/Warmth)."

Surya: "Correct. A man without a Mother has no foundation. A man without a Wife (Venus energy) has no roof. We have cleared the debt of the Mother and the Wife. The Chariot is lighter now. The heavy trunk is half-empty. But there is one more major debt. Perhaps the most painful one. The debt of the **Unborn Child**. The debt of the **Sister**. The debt of the **Cruelty to Nature**. We must now learn why the 'Fruit' (Children) sometimes rots on the vine. We must open the **Third Vault**. Turn the page to **Chapter 18**, where we will discuss the Science of Remediation—why Silver, Curd, and Cows actually work. We will decode the physics behind the magic."

PART VI: THE SCIENCE OF REMEDIATION

(The Physics of the Spirit)

CHAPTER 18: THE PHYSICS OF SILVER, CURD, AND COWS

(Decoding the Mechanics of the Remedy)

The Laboratory Of The Soul

The heavy iron doors of the Ancestral Ledger slammed shut, sealing away the ghosts of the past. The Chariot had left the dark mountain of Debts behind. The air, which had been thick with the dust of centuries and the smoke of regret, was now crystal clear. It vibrated with a strange, high-pitched hum—the sound of pure mathematics.

Aruna looked around. The landscape was no longer made of earth and stone. It was a grid of pure light. Geometric shapes floated in the ether—perfect squares of silver, rotating spheres of mercury, and pyramids of gold. The stars above were not distant points of light, but interconnected nodes in a vast, pulsating circuit.

Aruna: "O Surya, the journey has changed again. We have left the emotional storms of the Moon and the passionate fires of Venus. We have paid the debts of the past. But now, I feel a different kind of hunger. I want to know *how* it works. Why does throwing a piece of metal into a river change a man's destiny? Why does feeding a cow save a marriage? Why does burying a pot of honey stop a war in the bedroom? Is this magic, or is it a science I do not yet understand?"

Surya: "It is **Spiritual Physics**, Aruna. The universe is not made of stories; it is made of **Vibration**. Every object on Earth—a stone, a leaf, a metal, an animal—vibrates at a specific frequency. These frequencies correspond exactly to the frequencies of the planets. **Silver** vibrates at the frequency of the **Moon**. **Curd** vibrates at the frequency of **Venus**. **Copper** vibrates at the frequency of the **Sun**. When a Charioteer is sick, it means his internal frequency is out of tune. A remedy (*Upaya*) is simply the act of introducing a 'Tuning Fork' to correct the vibration. We are now entering the **Laboratory of the Red Book**. We will dismantle the rituals to see the machinery inside. We will strip away the superstition to find the science. We will learn why a **Square Piece of Silver** can stop a divorce, and why a **Black Cow** can absorb the heat of Mars. Prepare yourself. We are about to look under the hood of the Chariot."

The Physics Of Silver (Chandi)

(The Conductor of Peace)

The Material Properties Silver is the metal of the **Moon** (*Chandra*). In the periodic table of elements, Silver (Ag) has the highest electrical conductivity and the highest thermal conductivity of any metal. It is the ultimate **Conductor**. It moves energy rapidly. It does not hold heat; it dissipates it. It cools everything it touches. It reflects 95% of the visible light spectrum. It is a perfect mirror.

The Astrological Application In the *Lal Kitab*, Silver is used as a **Coolant** and a **Stabilizer**.

1. **Cooling the Heat (Mars/Sun):**
   - o *The Problem:* When a native has high blood pressure, anger issues, or fever (Mars afflictions), their internal "engine" is overheating.
   - o *The Remedy:* Drink water from a **Silver Tumbler**.
   - o *The Physics:* The silver ions infuse the water with 'Lunar Energy.' When the native drinks it, the 'Coolant' enters the bloodstream (Mars). It physically and energetically lowers the temperature of the blood. It acts as a radiator fluid for the body.
2. **Containing the Poison (Rahu/Saturn):**
   - o *The Problem:* When the mind is poisoned by anxiety (Rahu) or depression (Saturn), the thoughts are erratic and heavy.
   - o *The Remedy:* Keep a **Solid Silver Brick** in the house or pocket.
   - o *The Physics:* A solid block of silver acts as a 'Grounding

Weight.' It anchors the fluctuating mind. It provides a heavy, stable frequency that overrides the erratic noise of Rahu. It acts like a lightning rod, grounding the static electricity of anxiety.

The Mystery of the Square Piece One of the most famous and cryptic remedies in the Red Book is: **"Keep a Square Piece of Silver in the pocket."** Why square? Why not round?

- **Why Square?**
  - A Circle is **Mercury**. Mercury is movement, instability, and speed.
  - A Square is **Mars**. Mars is structure, stability, and earth. A square sits flat; it does not roll away.
- **Why Silver?**
  - Silver is **Moon**. Moon is water, fluid, and emotion.
- **The Alchemy:** When you shape Silver (Moon/Water) into a Square (Mars/Structure), you are creating a **Hybrid Element**. You are giving the 'Water' of the Moon a 'Container' of Mars.
- **The Function:** This remedy is used when the Moon is weak, 'fluid,' or under attack (e.g., Moon in 6th or 8th House). The 'Square' structure prevents the Moon energy from leaking away. It turns 'Water' into 'Ice.' It gives the native **Emotional Stability** and **Courage**. It forces the mind to hold its shape under pressure.

The Alchemy Of Curd (Dahi)

(The Fermented Venus)

The Transformation of Milk Milk is the **Moon**. It is pure, simple, white, and nurturing. It is the food of the infant. But when Milk is fermented, it changes state. Bacteria act upon it. It thickens. It becomes sour. It develops a skin. It becomes **Curd**. In the *Lal Kitab*, **Curd** represents **Venus** (*Shukra*). Why? Because Venus is the planet of **Transformation** and **Reproduction**. Just as milk transforms into curd through a biological process, the raw biological urge (Mars) transforms into refined love and beauty (Venus). Curd is also 'Earthier' than milk. It has substance. It is the "luxury" of milk.

The Remedial Application

1. **Bathing with Curd:**
   - *The Prescription:* "Rub curd on the body before bathing on Fridays."
   - *The Physics:* The skin is ruled by **Mercury** (texture) and **Venus** (beauty). By applying Curd (Venus) directly to the skin, you are feeding the 'Venusian Shield' of the body. The lactic acid chemically exfoliates (cleanses Rahu/Dirt) and moisturizes (adds Venus/Glow). It creates a bio-magnetic aura of attraction. You are wearing Venus.
2. **Eating Curd before a Journey:**
   - *The Tradition:* Eating 'Dahi-Shakkar' (Curd and Sugar) before leaving the house for important work.
   - *The Physics:*
     - Curd = **Venus.**
     - Sugar = **Mars** (Energy/Fuel).
     - Venus + Mars = **Passionate Action / Success.**
     - By ingesting this mixture, you are chemically programming your body for 'Victory' (Mars) and 'Gain' (Venus). You are fueling the Chariot for the road. You are combining "Desire" with "Energy."

The Prohibition:

- **Why not sell milk?** (Especially for Moon in 4th).
  - Selling milk drains the Moon. It sells the "Mother."
  - But selling **Curd** or **Ghee** is often permitted or less harmful. Why? Because you have added

'Value' (Venus) to it. You have transformed the raw material. You are trading a 'Product,' not the 'Source.' (Though for Moon in 4, even this is risky).

The Biology Of The Cow (Gau Mata)

(The Living Filter)

The Supreme Remedial Agent In the *Lal Kitab*, the **Cow** is not just an animal; she is a **Planetary Processing Unit**. She is a biological machine designed to transmute karma. She embodies **Venus** (The Earthly Mother) and **Moon** (The Milk Giver). But her anatomy is a map of the Zodiac:

- Her Horns: **Mars** (Defense).
- Her Mouth: **Rahu** (Consumption/Green Fodder).
- Her Tail: **Ketu** (Detachment/Swatting flies).
- Her Stomach: **Sun** (Digestion/Fire).
- Her Milk: **Moon** (Nourishment).
- Her Urine/Dung: **Ketu/Jupiter** (Purification/Gold).

The Mechanism of Feeding When a native feeds a Cow, a complex alchemical reaction occurs that cleanses his horoscope.

1. **The Input:** The native offers **Green Grass** (*Chara*).
   - Green Grass = **Mercury**.
2. **The Process:** The Cow takes the Mercury (Grass) into her Rahu (Mouth). She digests it with her Sun (Stomach).
3. **The Output:** She produces **Milk**.
   - Milk = **Moon**.
4. **The Equation: Mercury (Input) → Moon (Output).**
   - Normally, in the chart, Mercury and Moon are enemies. Mercury destroys Moon. Logic destroys Peace.
   - But the Cow **transmutes** the Enemy (Mercury) into the Friend (Moon).

  - o **The Result:** By feeding the cow, the native converts his 'Anxiety/Logic' (Mercury) into 'Peace/Wealth' (Moon). The Cow acts as a **Biological Filter** that removes the poison from the native's karma and returns nectar.

The 100 Cows Remedy (Stri Rin) Why feed 100 cows to cure the Wife's Debt?

- The Wife is **Venus.**
- The Debt is usually caused by **Rahu** (Abuse/Deceit) or **Sun** (Ego).
- When you feed 100 Cows, you are engaging the **Collective Power of Venus.**
- You are overwhelming the negative karma with a flood of positive, nurturing energy.
- The 'Breath' of the cow is said to cure lung diseases (Jupiter/ Mercury). The 'Touch' of the cow (stroking her back) calms the blood pressure (Mars).
- It is a **Holographic Remedy**. By healing the 'Macro-Wife' (Cow), you heal the 'Micro-Wife' (Spouse).

The Science Of Donation (Daan)

(The Physics of Displacement)

The Law of Transfer Donation in the *Lal Kitab* is not charity in the western sense; it is **Displacement**. Matter cannot be created or destroyed. Bad karma (Negative Energy) cannot just disappear. It must be moved. It must be transferred from the native's system to a place where it can be neutralized.

- **The Container:** When you donate an item (e.g., Black Urad Dal for Saturn), that item acts as a 'Container' for your negative Saturn energy. It absorbs the frequency of your suffering.
- **The Touch:** You must touch the item with your right hand (*Sankalp*). This creates a circuit. It transfers the vibration from your aura to the object.
- **The Recipient:** You give it to a beggar, a priest, or flow it in water.
    - If you give it to a **Beggar** (Saturn), he absorbs it. His system is designed to process Saturn energy; it sustains him.
    - If you flow it in **Water** (Moon), the vastness of the river dilutes the energy until it is harmless (Homeopathic dilution). The salt of your tear is lost in the ocean.
- **The Warning:** Never bring the container back. Once you have displaced the poison, looking back re-establishes the connection. You must walk away.

The 43-Day Cycle

(The Biological Clock)

Aruna: "Why 43 days, Surya? Why not 40 or 50? Why is this number so specific?"

Surya: "This is the **Rhythm of the Blood**, Aruna. The *Lal Kitab* is synced with human biology. In the human body, the red blood cells and the cellular memory renew in cycles. Specifically, it takes approximately **40 to 43 days** for a new habit or a new vibration to become permanent in the neural pathways and the bloodstream.

- **Day 1-10:** The Resistance Phase. The old karma fights back. The remedy feels heavy.
- **Day 11-30:** The Adaptation Phase. The body accepts the new frequency. The resistance fades.
- **Day 40-43:** The Locking Phase. The remedy becomes part of the DNA. The vibration stabilizes. If you break the cycle on Day 42, the memory resets. The wave collapses. You must start again. The 43 days ensure that the 'Tuning Fork' has struck the bell long enough for the bell to hold the note on its own."

Summary Of The Science

Aruna looked at the geometric shapes floating in the air. The Square Silver, the Pot of Curd, the Green Grass.

Aruna: "It is not magic, Surya. It is Engineering. We use **Shape** (Square/Round) to control structure. We use **Material** (Silver/Copper) to control frequency. We use **Biology** (Cows/Dogs) to transmute energy. We use **Time** (43 Days) to lock the program."

Surya: "Correct. You are no longer just a Charioteer; you are a

Mechanic of Destiny. You now possess the tools to fix the engine, cool the radiator, and heal the passengers. The Book of the Moon and Venus is complete. We have balanced the **Mind** and the **Desire**. But the road ahead is steep. We need **Power** to climb it. We need **Aggression**. We need **Fire**. The next volume waits for us. The **Red Flag** is flying on the horizon. We must summon the General. **End of Volume 2.** Prepare for **Volume 3: The Warrior's Shield**. We will learn the secrets of **Mars** and **Mercury**."

APPENDIX A: THE QUICK REFERENCE LEDGER

(Moon & Venus in the 12 Houses)

This ledger serves as a rapid diagnostic tool for the Charioteer. It distills the complex narratives of the *Lunar Tide* into their essential components: The Archetype, The Danger, and The Key Remedy.

Table I: The Moon (Chandra)

The Mind, The Mother, Liquid Cash, Peace

House	Archetype	The Danger	The Key Remedy
1st	The Cooling King	"Softness" leads to lack of ambition; drowning in empathy.	Red Handkerchief (Mars) in pocket. Avoid Green.
2nd	The Shiva Lingam	Hoarding wealth stops the flow; mistreating guests blocks income.	Feed Guests (Atithi Satkar). Bury Silver Brick.
3rd	The Green Moon	Anxiety, hallucinations, and conflict with siblings.	Sweet Water (Sherbat) to thirsty people. Silver Ring.
4th	The River of Plenty	Selling milk (Mother's essence) leads to poverty and mental illness.	Never Sell Milk. Public Water Dispenser (Pyaau).
5th	Water in the Desert	Greed or revealing secrets evaporates the luck; gambling destroys progeny.	White Handkerchief in pocket. Maintain Secrecy.
6th	Moon in the Deep Well	Depression, suicidal thoughts, absorbing others' trauma.	Serve Water at Cremation Ground/ Hospital. No Milk at Night.
7th	The Merchant of Emotion	Conflict between Mother and Wife; emotional trading leads to loss.	Weigh the Bride (Rice/Milk). Never trade in liquids.
8th	Moon in the Grave	Fear of death, depression, legacy trauma from mother.	Cremation Water in glass bottle at home. Silver Square.
9th	The Great Lake	Disrespecting elders or dirty altar turns the	Feed Snakes with milk. Saffron Tilak.

		ocean violent.	
10th	**The Frozen Lake**	**Emotional coldness; "King of Office, Beggar of Home."**	**No Milk at Night. Use/Trade Alcohol (do not drink).**
11th	**The Enemy's Court**	**Hunger for profit destroys peace; mother suffers.**	**Kheer to Bhairon Temple. Gold on body.**
12th	**Rainwater on Roof**	**Saving money causes loss; hoarding leads to insomnia.**	**Saunf (Aniseed) under pillow. Drink rainwater.**

Table Ii: Venus (Shukra)

The Wife, Desire, Luxury, Semen

House	Archetype	The Danger	The Key Remedy
1st	The Burning Flower	Early marriage (before 25) burns the career and health.	Black Cow service. Curd bath. Marry after 25.
2nd	The Clay of Creation	Adultery turns gold to dust; disrespecting labor ruins wealth.	Potatoes/Turmeric to temple. Blue Flower in earth.
3rd	The Siren in the Jungle	Flirting/Scandals destroy luck (9th); musical instruments trigger fights.	Respect Women. Silver jewelry for spouse.
4th	The Two Wives	Wife vs. Mother conflict; addiction; two marriages.	Remarriage Ritual with wife. Copper Coin in river.
5th	The Padmini	Passion destroys Career (Sun); love affairs cause scandal.	Clean Ancestral Altar. Feed Cows. Marry the lover.
6th	The Barefoot Beauty	Wife's illness drains wealth; debt due to lifestyle.	Gold Clip in wife's hair. Wife must wear shoes.
7th	The Bronze Idol	Pride in partner destroys income; partner becomes cold/demanding.	Blue Flower in mud. Bronze utensils out of bedroom.
8th	The Burning Chariot	Secret affairs lead to ruin; wife's health suffers.	Blue Flower in dirty drain. Copper Coin in pyre.

9th	**The Saffron Lady**	**Laziness stops the luck; "Easy Money" curses the family.**	**Silver Square under Neem tree. Hard Work.**
10th	**The Wall of Clay**	**Blindness to wife's pain; career success at cost of home.**	**Build & Destroy Mud Wall. West wall strong.**
11th	**The Oil of Luxury**	**"Slippery" wealth; friends betray; social life hurts children.**	**Mustard Oil donation. Cotton wicks.**
12th	**The Bed of Roses**	**Miserliness brings thorns; wife becomes sickly/detached.**	**Wife buries Blue Flower. Donate Cows.**

Note: This ledger is a summary. For the full alchemical logic and diagnostic stories, refer to the respective chapters in the main text.

APPENDIX B: THE "ARTIFICIAL PLANETS" TABLE

(The Masnui Grah Reference Code)

In the *Lal Kitab*, planetary energies are not static. When specific planets sit together (or aspect each other), they chemically combine to create a **Third Energy** known as a *Masnui Grah* (Artificial Planet).

This table is the **Chemist's Cheat Sheet**. It allows the Charioteer to diagnose the *Resultant Force* in a chart, rather than just reading the individual planets.

Table I: The Benefic Mixtures

(Combinations that Create Life & Resource)

Ingredients (Planet A + Planet B)	The Result (Artificial Planet)	The Concept	The Implication for the Native
Sun + Jupiter	**MOON**	**The Pious Soul**	Authority + Wisdom = Peace of Mind. This combination rectifies a weak Moon in the chart.
Sun + Venus	**JUPITER**	**The Royal Guru**	The King + The Wife = Wisdom. This creates "Dharma" and high status, though it may burn the wife's health.
Jupiter + Rahu	**MERCURY (Benefic)**	**The Intelligent Expansion**	Wisdom + Obsession = Genius Intellect. This creates a brilliant, strategic mind (if Jupiter is strong).
Mars + Venus	**MOON (Active)**	**The Passionate Current**	Fire + Semen = Vitality. This creates intense creative or sexual energy. It fuels the "River" of life.
Mercury + Venus	**SUN (Artificial)**	**The Gandharva**	Intellect + Beauty = Charisma. This creates an "Artificial Sun"—fame, eloquence, and social power.
Rahu + Ketu	**VENUS**	**The Dragon's Breath**	Ambition + Execution = Luxury. The two nodes combined (via aspect) manifest material desire.

Table Ii: The Malefic Mixtures

(Combinations that Create Poison or Obstruction)

Ingredients (Planet A + Planet B)	The Result (Artificial Planet)	The Concept	The Implication for the Native
Moon + Saturn	**KETU (Malefic)**	**The Poisoned Milk**	Mind + Darkness = Depression/Void. This destroys peace and creates phobias (Vish Yoga).
Moon + Mercury	**SATURN (Malefic)**	**The Agitated Water**	Emotion + Logic = Anxiety/Suicide. The mind turns against itself. It creates "Foam."
Sun + Saturn	**RAHU (Malefic)**	**The Eclipse**	Soul + Darkness = Confusion. This creates deep insecurity and conflict with authority.
Mars + Mercury	**SATURN (Prison)**	**The Muted Weapon**	Courage + Logic = Frustration. The native has energy but cannot express it. The "Lion in the Cage."
Venus + Rahu	**MARS (Bad)**	**The Smoky Mirror**	Love + Obsession = Scandal. This creates destructive passion and bad reputation.
Jupiter + Ketu	**MOON (Weak)**	**The Lonely Guru**	Wisdom + Detachment = Isolation. The native has wisdom but no emotional connection.

Table Iii: The Remedial Equations

(How to Create a Missing Planet)

If a specific planet is missing or weak in the chart, you can "manufacture" its energy by using its component parts.

Target Planet (To Create)	The Remedy (Action)	The Logic
To Create MOON	Wear **Gold** (Jupiter) on the **Body** (Sun).	Sun + Jupiter = Moon.
To Create SUN	Speak with **Eloquence** (Mercury) and dress **Well** (Venus).	Mercury + Venus = Sun.
To Create JUPITER	Respect the **Father** (Sun) and the **Wife** (Venus).	Sun + Venus = Jupiter.
To Create MARS	Combine **Authority** (Sun) with **Responsibility** (Saturn).	Sun + Saturn = Mars (High Energy).
To Create MERCURY	Combine **Wisdom** (Jupiter) with **Strategy** (Rahu).	Jupiter + Rahu = Mercury.

Note: These equations are the hidden grammar of the Red Book. Do not apply them mechanically. Always check the "Landlord" of the house where the mixture occurs (see Chapter 15).

APPENDIX C: THE GUIDE TO BLIND PLANETS

(Diagnosing the Andha Grah)

In the *Lal Kitab*, the 10th House is not just the house of Career; it is the **Eye of the Chart**. It represents the native's ability to see the path ahead.

However, certain planetary combinations in the 10th House create a condition known as **Andha Teva** (Blind Chart) or **Andha Grah** (Blind Planet). This blindness is not physical; it is karmic. The native has power (10th House) but no vision.

I. The Mechanism Of Blindness

The 10th House vs. The 4th House

- **The 10th House:** The Throne, The Career, The Father, The Government (Noon).
- **The 4th House:** The Home, The Mother, The Peace, The Water (Midnight).

In the *Lal Kitab*, the 10th House looks directly at the 4th House. If two **Enemy Planets** sit together in the 10th House, they create a "Smoke" of conflict. This smoke rises and blinds the planets in the 10th House. More importantly, because the 10th House looks at the 4th, this "Smoke" fills the 4th House (Home). **Result:** The native is successful in the world (10th) but miserable at home (4th). He is "Blind" to his own happiness.

Ii. The Blind Combinations (In The 10th House)

Not all conjunctions cause blindness. Only the meeting of **Bitter Enemies** creates the smoke.

The Conflict (Planets in 10th)	The Blindness Effect	The Symptom
SUN + SATURN	**The Dark King**	The native doubts his own authority. He is suspicious of his father and government. He works hard but gets no credit.
MOON + SATURN	**The Frozen Eye**	Deep pessimism. The native cannot see the "Good" in anything. Chronic depression. The

		mother suffers.
MARS + SATURN	**The Mad Elephant**	Uncontrollable rage followed by paralysis. The native destroys his own career in a fit of anger.
SUN + RAHU	**The Eclipsed Throne**	Confusion about identity. The native is easily manipulated by others. Scandal in career.
MOON + KETU	**The Clouded Mirror**	Total lack of intuition. The native makes the wrong decision every time. Emotional detachment.

Iii. The Diagnostic Test

To confirm if a planet is truly "Blind," check the **4th House**.

- **Rule:** If the 10th House has enemy planets, AND the 4th House is **Empty** or Afflicted, the blindness is confirmed.
- **Exception:** If the 4th House has a **Friendly Planet** (e.g., Moon in 4th while Sun+Saturn are in 10th), the "Mother" saves the "Child." The blindness is cured by the 4th House planet.

Iv. The Cure For Blindness

You cannot separate the planets in the 10th House. You must treat the **Symptom** (The Blindness).

1. The Remedy of the 10 Blind People:

- **Action:** Feed 10 blind people on a single day.
- **Logic:** By serving the "Blind," you acknowledge the karma. You pay the debt of sight. This acts as a "Lantern" for the chart.

2. The Remedy of the Dark Room:

- **Action:** Keep a room in the house dark (or use dark curtains) in the West direction.
- **Logic:** This honors Saturn (Darkness). It prevents the Sun (Light) from irritating the Saturn energy in the home.

3. The Copper Coin (For Sun+Saturn):

- **Action:** Wear a Copper Coin around the neck.
- **Logic:** This lifts the Sun out of the 10th House (Feet/Knees) and places it in the 1st House (Neck/Head). It separates the King from the Coal Mine.

Note: A Blind Chart is not a death sentence. It is a warning. The native must walk slowly, use a stick (Caution), and trust the advice of others (The Guide).

EPILOGUE

AFTER THE TIDE HAS PASSED

The Chariot stops at the edge of a great, still lake.The water holds the sky perfectly. Above and below, the same stars.

Aruna lets the reins fall slack. For the first time since the journey began, he does not look ahead. He looks down—into the water, at his own reflection. He has aged in ways that have nothing to do with years. He has the eyes of a man who has sat with both the Kings who weep and the sages who do not.

Behind him lies the full territory of the Lunar Tide. The twelve chambers of the Moon, each a different register of the same ancient ache—the need to feel at home in the world, to be nourished, to be held. The twelve stations of Venus, each a different grammar of the same irreducible hunger—to desire and to be desired, to create something beautiful before the body returns to the earth.

He has learned that Peace is not a virtue but a chemistry. That Love is not a mystery but a mechanics. That the rituals of the Lal Kitab—the silver square, the buried blue flower, the hundred cows, the forty-three days of unbroken intention—are not the superstitions of frightened men but the technology of a civilization that once understood the physics of the invisible.

"Surya," he says, his voice quieter than it has been all journey. "I came to this volume looking for answers about the Moon and Venus in a horoscope. But I find I am leaving with a different question entirely."

"Ask it," Surya says.

"We have spoken much of the debts—the Matri Rin, the Stri Rin, the Pitri Rin. The inherited wounds. The karma passed down like furniture no one wanted but no one threw away. My question is this: when we pay these debts—when we perform the remedies, when we honor the ancestors, when we repair the Moon and strengthen the Venus—are we healing ourselves? Or are we healing the ones who come after us?"

Surya is silent for a long time. When he speaks, his voice carries that particular resonance of a thing that has always been true but is rarely said aloud.

"Both," he says simply. "The river does not choose who it irrigates. It only chooses to flow."

Aruna nods. He understands now what the Lal Kitab's deeper instruction is. Not just "fix your chart." But: become someone whose chart the next generation does not have to fix. Become the ancestor who paid his debts. The father whose son wakes without the ancestral fear in his chest. The husband who repaired the Stri Rin so completely that his daughter inherits a chart full of grace.

This is the hidden ambition of the Red Book. Not to predict fate, but to interrupt it. Not to diagnose suffering, but to teach the art of its voluntary end.

The Moon, when healthy, is the coolant in the engine of a life. It allows the Sun to burn without scorching. It allows the ambition to drive without destroying. It allows the Kings to sit on their thrones without the night terror of an empty court.

Venus, when clear, is the proof that the body's intelligence was correct all along—that it was right to hunger, right to reach, right to want the beautiful and the sweet and the warm. Venus, unafflicted, is the permission the soul has been waiting for.

Together, the Moon and Venus form what the Red Book calls the Lunar Tide: the great inner rhythm of feeling and desire that runs beneath the visible architecture of a life. You can have the finest Chariot in the world. You can have the most disciplined horses, the sharpest wheels, the most authoritative driver. But without the Tide, the Chariot goes nowhere. It stands gleaming in the sun, perfectly engineered, perfectly still.
May your Tide be strong.

May your Moon rise over a shore that is not afraid of the water.

May your Venus bloom in the house that suits her best.

The next volume waits on the horizon. The Red Flag is flying. The General is sharpening his sword. Volume 3 will enter the forge of Mars and the labyrinth of Mercury—the twin forces of Aggression and Intelligence that determine how we fight and how we think. But that is another journey.

For now, the lake is still. The Chariot rests. And the stars above and below are identical.

The Charioteer smiles at his own reflection.

He has learned to recognize peace when he sees it.

www.ingramcontent.com/pod-product-compliance
Lightning Source LLC
LaVergne TN
LVHW030910080826
845145LV00010B/2845